*A powerful memoir of resilience, faith,
and healing from childhood trauma*

Hope in the
Darkness
Finding God's Light

MISTY FIELDS

Copyright © 2025 Misty Fields.

All rights reserved.

No part of this publication may be reproduced, distributed or transmitted in any form or by any means, including photocopying, recording or other electronic or mechanical methods, without the prior written permission of the publisher, except in the case of brief quotations, reviews and other noncommercial uses permitted by copyright law.

Contents

Author's Note v
Introduction. A Story of Survival, Redemption,
       and Hope vii

Chapter 1. A Childhood Shaped by Love and Loss 1
Chapter 2. The Breaking Point & Finding God
                in the Chaos 7
Chapter 3. Holding On Through the Fog 13
Chapter 4. The Nights We Were Left Alone 18
Chapter 5. Nowhere to Hide 25
Chapter 6. The Night We Fled. 30
Chapter 7. Wanting to Be Wanted 34
Chapter 8. Betrayed and Broken. 38
Chapter 9. Back to Kentucky. .43
Chapter 10. A Father's Return. .48
Chapter 11. A New Home, A New Reality 53
Chapter 12. Running from the Pain. 58
Chapter 13. Left Behind, But Not Forgotten. 64
Chapter 14. Searching for Love in the Wrong Places. . . .70

Chapter 15. Finding My Own Way 75
Chapter 16. A Love I Had Prayed For 79
Chapter 17. A Grief I Never Expected 84
Chapter 18. A Love Too Strong to Ignore 89
Chapter 19. Miracles and Heartaches 95
Chapter 20. A Love Worth Celebrating 101
Chapter 21. Faith, Family, and a Business Built on
             Prayer 106
Chapter 22. Healing, Home, and the Journey in
             Between 112
Chapter 23. When Love Isn't Enough 118
Chapter 24. The Sister I Couldn't Save 123
Chapter 25. Carried Through the Breaking 128
Chapter 26. Letting Go of the Hurt 133
Chapter 27. Peace in the Aftermath 137
Chapter 28. A Call to Know Christ 142

Epilogue. She Made It 147
Acknowledgments 149

Author's Note

Thank you for taking the time to read my story.

Writing Hope in the Darkness: Finding God's Light was not simply about telling what happened. It was about facing it. It meant revisiting the places I once tried to outrun, naming the pain for what it was, and acknowledging the ways God was present even when I could not see Him clearly.

This book is deeply personal. It holds memories of trauma, instability, addiction, grief, and seasons where survival felt like the only goal. But it also holds something stronger than all of that — redemption. Not because I handled everything well, and not because the pain wasn't real, but because God never stopped pursuing me through it.

I wrote this for those who feel unseen. For the ones who had to grow up too fast. For the mothers who are raising children while still healing their own wounds. For anyone who has ever wondered if their past disqualified them from peace. I know what it feels like to carry responsibility too young, to long for stability, and to wrestle with both faith and disappointment at the same time.

If that is you, I want you to know this: your story is not over. What happened to you may shape you, but it does not have to define you. God is not intimidated by your past. He is not shocked by your wounds. He is steady, patient, and present — even in the chapters that feel the darkest.

My prayer is not that you see me in these pages. It is that you see Him. That you recognize His faithfulness in places you once thought were abandoned. That you find courage to face your own healing. And that you leave these pages believing that generational cycles can be broken, that restoration is possible, and that Jesus still redeems what feels ruined.

If He could carry me through every chapter you are about to read, I believe He can carry you too.

With love and faith,
Misty Fields

Introduction

A Story of Survival, Redemption, and Hope

For many years, I carried my story quietly. Not because it did not matter, but because I was not sure anyone wanted to hear it. Trauma has a way of convincing you that silence is safer. It tells you that your pain is too messy, too complicated, or too shameful to bring into the light. So I learned to function. I learned to survive. I learned to carry memories that shaped me long before I understood what they meant.

This book is not simply a collection of hard stories. It is the account of a childhood shaped by addiction, abuse, instability, and betrayal, and the slow, steady work of God in the middle of it all. I did not grow up in safety. I grew up learning how to read moods, protect siblings, endure violence, and carry secrets. I grew up believing that love could disappear without warning. But even in those years, when I did not recognize His hand, God was present.

There were seasons when survival was the only goal. Seasons when I questioned my worth. Seasons when I searched for love in places that only deepened the wounds. I made choices out of pain. I trusted people who should never have been trusted. I believed lies about myself that took years to unlearn. Yet even in those decisions, even in my rebellion and confusion, God did not turn away from me.

This is not a story about pretending everything worked out easily. It is a story about what it looks like when grace meets brokenness. It is about how trauma can shape you but does not have to define you. It is about how the very places that felt like disqualification became the places God chose to redeem.

If you have ever felt unseen, this book is for you. If you grew up too fast and learned to hold everything together while falling apart inside, this book is for you. If addiction has touched your family, if abuse has marked your past, if abandonment has shaped your identity, I want you to know that I understand the weight of those experiences. I also want you to know that they are not the final word over your life.

Scripture became an anchor for me long before I fully understood it. "The Lord himself goes before you and will be with you; he will never leave you nor forsake you. Do not be afraid; do not be discouraged." — Deuteronomy 31:8. I did not always feel brave. I did not always feel strong. But I was never alone.

There were years when I wondered if I was too damaged to be used by God. I believed the lie that my past had permanently disqualified me. Over time, I came to understand that the very wounds I wanted to hide were the places He wanted to heal. "The Lord is close to the brokenhearted and saves those who are crushed in spirit." — Psalm 34:18. He was close to me long before I knew how to be close to Him.

I am writing this for the ones who feel responsible for everyone else. For the women who have carried families while trying to heal themselves. For the ones who smile in public and cry in private. For the ones who wonder if peace is possible for someone with a history like theirs.

This book is my testimony, not because I did everything right, but because God never stopped pursuing me. His grace sustained me through addiction in my family, through abuse that tried to silence me, through courtrooms that disappointed me, and through seasons when I did not know who I was anymore. He carried me when I did not have the strength to carry myself.

"For I know the plans I have for you," declares the Lord, "plans to prosper you and not to harm you, plans to give you hope and a future." — Jeremiah 29:11.

My hope is that as you turn these pages, you will begin to see your own story differently. Not as a collection of broken pieces, but as a life still being written. There is healing. There is freedom. And there is real, lasting hope through Jesus Christ.

This is my story. And I believe God is still writing yours.

Chapter 1

A Childhood Shaped by Love and Loss

My sister Mandy was only eleven months younger than me. We were so close in age that we felt more like twins than sisters. From the time we could walk, we did everything together. We did not have much, but we had each other. In a childhood marked by instability, that bond meant everything.

My earliest memories are wrapped in the warmth of our paternal grandparents' home. Mandy and I spent so much time there that it felt more like home than anywhere else. She would curl up in Pawpaw's arms, completely at peace, while I lay next to our grandmother, who we affectionately called Mother. Life at their house had a steady rhythm. It was safe. Predictable. Full of love.

There was a simple reason we were there so often. Our parents were usually gone. Nights at the bar were more common than nights at home, and Pawpaw and Mother quietly stepped in to raise us. As little girls, we did not see the brokenness behind that arrangement. We only knew we were loved.

Pawpaw owned a logging business, and sometimes he would take us along to check job sites. I loved riding in his truck, watching the world pass by. But Saturdays were the best. Every week we went to Hardee's for fresh biscuits, then stopped at the gas station so we could each pick out a Yoo-hoo and a Moon Pie. Those small routines felt magical. Looking back, I realize they were not extravagant. They were intentional. That is what made them special.

Pawpaw was a strong man, shaped by years of hard labor. But with us, he was gentle and patient. The only time I remember disappointing him was during one of those truck rides. He warned me not to touch the window because it would not stay up without the wedge. The moment he stepped away, curiosity won. I pulled it out. When he returned and saw it, his voice was firm but never harsh. Even in correction, I felt safe. That feeling stayed with me.

Mother was just as much a part of our world. She owned an antique store and often brought home discarded furniture to restore. I would sit and watch her sand rough edges and breathe life back into pieces others had thrown away. I did not know it then, but I was watching restoration.

Years later, I would recognize that same process in my own life.

Evenings followed a familiar pattern. Pawpaw came home in his heavy work boots, settled into his recliner, and soaked his tired feet. We gathered around the television while peace settled over the house. In the background, Mother hummed old hymns. Her favorite was "One Day at a Time, Sweet Jesus." Sometimes she sang while cooking. Sometimes she closed her eyes and hummed softly under her breath. I did not fully understand the words, but they settled deep inside me. God's presence became something I associated with safety and home.

Sundays belonged to Mother. She always took us to a small Pentecostal church with wooden pews and a preacher whose energy filled the room. He was older, but you would never guess it by the way he moved, shouting and pacing the aisles, sometimes even climbing on the pews to make his point. One Sunday, after the church reached a record attendance, he preached from the roof. As a child, it felt wild and overwhelming, but it also felt alive. I did not understand theology, but I understood hope. That church was full of it.

Mandy was strong-willed from the beginning. Her tantrums could last for hours, lying on the floor and screaming with everything in her. But no matter how fierce the storm, only one person could calm her. Pawpaw would scoop her up, whisper in her ear, and she would melt against him. He called her "Nanny Cat." She was his baby girl, and he was her safe place.

Sometimes I wish I could freeze those moments. The Saturday biscuits. The sweetness of Yoo-hoos. The sound of hymns drifting through the house. The strength of Pawpaw's arms around us. But life does not freeze. It moves forward. And sometimes it breaks.

I was four and a half years old when everything changed.

That morning began like any other. We were home with our parents. My dad, who worked for Pawpaw, had not gone into work. He was still in bed, hungover from the night before.

Then the phone rang.

I can still picture it hanging on the hallway wall. I remember my mother answering it and watching her face crumble. She dropped the receiver and ran to wake my dad. Through sobs, she said the words that split our world in two. Pawpaw was gone.

There had been an accident at work. He was driving heavy equipment across a narrow bridge when something malfunctioned. The machine plunged into the river below. It was February, and the water was ice cold. His heavy boots and clothing pulled him down. My uncle and cousin jumped in after him, but he shouted for them to stop and save themselves.

They said he suffered a massive heart attack in those freezing waters.

I did not understand death, but I understood devastation. I watched my father collapse under the weight of it, shouting "No" over and over. In his anguish, he punched a hole in the wall. He blamed himself. If only he had gone to work that day.

Pawpaw was deeply loved, not just by us but by everyone who knew him. His funeral was the largest I have ever attended. Two services were held, one in Illinois and another in Tennessee. So many people came that my uncle rented limousines for the procession. Pawpaw was laid to rest in our family cemetery. With him, a part of my childhood was buried too.

Grief does not just take a person. It removes the foundation they built. Without Pawpaw's steady presence, everything began to shift. Our family slowly unraveled. Mandy and I were too young to understand it fully, but we felt it. The security we had known was replaced with confusion, instability, and pain.

Looking back now, I see that day as the dividing line of my childhood. Before his death, life felt warm and full of song. Afterward, it felt uncertain and heavy.

But even in that darkness, something remained.

God.

I could not see Him clearly then. I only knew that the house felt quieter. The hymns felt farther away. The laughter did not echo the same.

The foundation had cracked.

And when a foundation cracks, everything built on top of it begins to shift.

What I did not know at four and a half years old was that this would only be the first loss. The first unraveling. The first time life would teach me that love and grief often walk hand in hand.

But even then, before I had language for faith, God was already writing a story I would one day understand.

Chapter 2

The Breaking Point & Finding God in the Chaos

G rief doesn't just take a person. It takes everything they were holding together.

When Pawpaw died, it wasn't only the loss of my grandfather. It was the loss of the foundation that kept our family steady. His presence had been shelter. His strength had been stability. Without him, everything began to shift.

My dad unraveled.

He had always struggled with alcohol and drugs, but after Pawpaw was gone, whatever control he had left seemed to disappear. As a little girl, I did not understand addiction or grief. I just knew the man who once worked beside his father now seemed lost. The house felt different. Colder. Tense in ways I could not explain.

The warmth I had known at my grandparents' home was gone. Home became unpredictable. Some days were loud with arguments. Other days were quiet in a way that felt just as frightening. I learned early to read the room. To watch faces. To listen for tone.

Even at five years old, I could feel that something had broken.

One night, that brokenness became impossible to ignore.

My dad stormed out of my grandmother's house carrying one of her antique lamps. I remember Mother following him to the door, her voice shaking as she pleaded, "Dean, please. No."

But addiction is louder than love.

He took me and Mandy with him that night. I did not know where we were going. I only knew it was somewhere we had never been before. The streets looked unfamiliar. The houses were close together and dimly lit.

"Stay down," he told us.

I slid onto the floorboard of the car, my cheek pressed against the cool leather. Mandy was beside me. We whispered to each other at first, then stopped altogether. The night felt heavy. I remember staring at the bottom of the seat in front of me and wishing we were back at Pawpaw's house.

When the car doors flew open again, everything felt different.

I looked up.

He was covered in blood.

It was on his hands, his face, his shirt. I did not understand what had happened. I only knew it was wrong.

"Go!" he shouted at my mom.

She drove.

"Stay down. Don't look at me," he barked again.

But I had already looked.

That image stayed with me. Not just the blood, but the fear in his eyes. As a child, I could not process what I had seen. I just carried it inside me.

After that night, something in me changed. I became more alert. More watchful. I learned that danger could arrive without warning.

It did not take long before it showed up again.

One afternoon, flashing blue lights filled the road behind us. I remember the way the colors reflected inside the car. I waited for my dad to pull over.

He did not.

Instead, he pressed harder on the gas.

The car sped forward, faster and faster. I gripped the seat and tried not to cry. I did not scream. I did not move. I just froze.

Suddenly he slammed on the brakes, jumped out of the driver's seat, and ran.

He left me there.

I remember sitting alone in the back seat, my heart pounding in my ears. A police officer opened the door and gently lifted me out. His voice was calm. His hands were steady. That was the first time I realized that not all authority felt frightening.

I was taken to the station while they searched for my mom. My dad was arrested. But even then, it did not feel like an ending. It felt like a pause before the next storm.

The next time came sooner than I expected.

He was driving a logging truck with all of us inside when the blue lights appeared again. I remember the size of that truck, how high off the ground we felt. He turned onto a narrow road bordered by steep embankments. The truck rocked as it moved. I could feel the fear rising in my chest.

When he realized he could not outrun them, he made my mom take the wheel and ran into the woods.

This time, he did not escape.

He was sent to prison.

And I was still only five years old.

When the house grew quiet after that, it was not peaceful. It was empty. The chaos had been loud, but the absence felt just as heavy.

As a child, I did not have words for what I felt. I only knew that the world no longer felt stable. The man I loved had become someone unpredictable. The safety I once knew had been replaced with uncertainty.

But in the middle of that confusion, something small began to grow.

A quiet awareness.

I did not fully understand God yet. I could not explain faith. But I remembered hymns. I remembered safety.

I remembered that there was something bigger than the chaos in my house.

Looking back now, I see His protection everywhere.

In the police officer who carried me from the car.

In the fact that we survived the speeding roads.

In the narrow escapes that could have ended differently.

At five years old, I could not explain resilience. I could not explain grace. But I was living under both.

I did not understand why my dad was so broken or what drove him to numb his pain. I only understood the fear that followed him. And deep down, I sensed something else. There had to be more than this. There had to be a reason I was still standing.

God never left me, even when everything else felt unstable. He saw me. He carried me through moments I was too young to process. And as much as my father's choices hurt us, I believe God never stopped pursuing him either.

Addiction blinds people. It convinces them they are beyond redemption. My dad tried to outrun his pain. He buried it instead of healing it.

But no one can run forever.

Eventually the running stops.

Eventually you face what you have been avoiding.

Prison slowed my father down. Inside those walls, he often turned to God. He would read his Bible. He would pray. He would talk about wanting to change. I believe those moments were real. I believe his heart wanted to be different.

But structure can hold a man together in ways freedom cannot. Outside those walls, the same pain waited. The same patterns. And although he reached for God more than once, staying free was a battle he could not seem to win.

As a child, that was hard to understand. How could someone love God and still lose to addiction? I did not have the words for it then. I only knew two things at once. I was afraid of him. And I loved him.

Both were true.

Even in the chaos. Even in the confusion. I loved my dad.

And I still believed that God was not finished writing his story.

Chapter 3

Holding On Through the Fog

The day we visited my dad in prison felt like a rare bright spot in a season that had grown heavy and uncertain. I was only five years old, and so much had changed in such a short time that I could barely understand what was happening around me. Life after his arrest felt quieter, but the quiet did not bring peace. It brought absence. It brought questions no one knew how to answer.

My mom was pregnant when my dad went to prison, and he knew about the baby before he left. That made the separation feel even heavier. By the time we went to see him, my baby sister had already been born. In the middle of everything that felt broken, her tiny life felt like something new to hold onto. She was a reminder that even when things fall apart, life continues moving forward.

The night before the visit, my mom rolled our hair and laid out matching dresses. I remember sensing how important it was to her that we looked nice. Even though we were going to a prison, she treated it like something meaningful. In her own way, she was trying to protect a piece of normalcy for us.

The prison felt different from the jails I had seen before. The metal detectors, the guards, the waiting rooms all felt more serious. When we finally walked into the visitation area and sat at the cold table, my heart pounded. I did not know what to expect. I did not know if he would look different or feel different.

Then I saw him.

His face lit up the moment he saw us. That familiar smile spread across his face, and for a moment, everything else faded away. I ran into his arms without hesitation. In that brief embrace, I felt like I had my dad back. Not the broken version. Not the angry version. Just my dad.

Those visits were short, but they mattered. Even after everything, my love for him did not change. I clung to the good memories. The warmth of his hugs. The way he kissed my forehead. The sound of his laughter when he was sober and present. Those were the parts of him I chose to hold onto.

Leaving that day was the hardest part. I cried most of the drive home, staring out the window and hoping somehow this was temporary. I did not understand charges or court systems. I only understood that my dad was not coming home with us.

As I grew older, my feelings toward him became more complicated. Especially after I became a mother myself. I would look at my children and feel a fierce protectiveness rise inside me. Their safety was not negotiable. Their well-being came before everything. And I struggled to understand how addiction had ever felt stronger than love.

Over time, though, I began to see something I could not grasp as a child. My dad always turned back to God in prison. He read his Bible. He prayed. He talked about change. His heart wanted to be different. He was not incapable of remorse. He was not blind to the damage. But once he was released, the same patterns and pressures pulled him back under. The structure of prison removed temptation. The outside world brought it back. His desire to change was real, but his ability to stay free was fragile.

That realization brought both compassion and heartbreak. I could see that he was broken long before he broke us. Addiction had wrapped itself tightly around his life. Even when he reached for God, he struggled to hold onto that surrender once he stepped outside those prison walls.

After he went away, life felt like walking through thick fog. Nothing felt steady. My mom tried her best to hold us together. She signed up for government assistance, and I remember standing in long lines beside her waiting for boxes of food. Blocks of cheese. Jars of peanut butter.

Powdered milk. The food helped, but it was a constant reminder that things had changed.

We were surviving, but everything felt fragile.

I started kindergarten during that time, hoping school might bring some sense of stability. Instead, I acted out constantly. I could not sit still. I struggled to listen. I spent more time in time-out than I did learning. Looking back now, I understand what I could not name then. I was angry. Angry that Pawpaw was gone. Angry that my dad was in prison. Angry that everything that once felt safe had disappeared.

Around that same time, extended family was often around, and that should have brought comfort. Instead, it brought confusion. One of my older male cousins began isolating me when no one was watching. Sometimes it was in dark closets. Sometimes between clothing racks at my grandmother's shop. He would press himself against me while we were still clothed. I did not understand what was happening. I did not know it was wrong. I only knew that my body would freeze.

I did not fight. I did not tell anyone. I did not even have the words.

That is what trauma does to a child. It silences them before they understand why they are silent.

I carried it quietly, assuming that if I did not speak about it, maybe it would stop. But silence does not erase pain. It buries it. And the longer I stayed quiet, the smaller I felt.

Now, as an adult, I wish I could go back and hold that little girl. I would tell her she did nothing wrong. That freezing was not weakness. That shame never belonged to her.

At the time, though, I only knew that everything felt uncertain.

And yet, even in that fog, God was there.

He was there in the prison visitation room when I ran into my dad's arms. He was there in the government lines. He was there in the silence no one else noticed. He saw what I could not say. He heard what I could not pray.

"You keep track of all my sorrows. You have collected all my tears in your bottle. You have recorded each one in your book." — Psalm 56:8

Even when my world felt unstable, even when I felt small and unseen, I was not invisible to Him.

I was holding on, even when I did not realize it.

Chapter 4

The Nights We Were Left Alone

When my dad came home from prison, it felt like a second chance. After months of absence, our family was under one roof again. For a little while, life felt almost normal. We moved a couple of hours away from my grandmother, and I started first grade in a new school. My dad found work out of town, and my mom stayed home with us. In the afternoons, she would make me a fried bologna sandwich after school, and for a brief season, we settled into something that resembled stability.

Our new neighborhood had other children, and Mandy and I finally had a place where we could ride our bikes and play without constantly looking over our shoulders. We spent hours in the parking lot across the street, laughing and pretending to be like everyone else.

I wanted to believe we had turned a corner. I wanted to believe prison had changed him.

But old patterns have a way of resurfacing.

It started slowly. He began coming home later than usual. Then he started coming home drunk. At first, I tried to convince myself it was temporary. He was working. He was home. Maybe this time it would not spiral. I clung to that hope longer than I should have.

Then one night, my mom left with him.

The baby was asleep when they walked out the door. Mandy and I stayed home. I do not remember how old I was exactly, but I remember the weight of responsibility settling on me as soon as the door shut. At some point during the night, my baby sister woke up crying. She would not stop. I climbed into her crib and saw her empty bottle. I knew she was hungry.

I dragged a chair across the kitchen floor and pushed it up to the counter. My hands were small, but I had watched my mom make formula enough times to imitate the process. I scooped the powder, poured the water, and shook the bottle carefully. Then I climbed back over the crib railing and placed it in her mouth. She drank quietly and eventually fell back asleep.

I should have felt proud. Instead, I felt older.

Before I could settle back into bed, Mandy appeared in the doorway. Her face was pale.

"I see blue lights," she whispered.

My heart dropped. Red and blue flashes filled the room through the window. Then came the knock. Loud. Firm. Demanding.

We froze.

We had been told never to open the door for anyone. That rule had been drilled into us. So we stayed silent. We did not move. We barely breathed. Eventually the lights disappeared, and the knocking stopped. Whoever had come left.

But the fear did not.

When my parents finally returned, I pretended to be asleep. I did not ask questions. I did not mention the police. I did not tell them about making the bottle. I had already learned that handling things quietly was safer than drawing attention.

That night was not an exception. It became a pattern.

More and more, we were left alone. Two little girls and a baby, trying to manage responsibilities we were too young to carry. Each night added a new layer of anxiety. I listened for every sound. I learned to sleep lightly. I learned that childhood could be interrupted at any moment.

Then my mom had another baby. And before we could adjust, my dad made another sudden decision. We were moving to Alabama.

There was no long discussion. No preparation. Just packing and leaving again.

The move felt less like opportunity and more like escape. My dad rented a small block building with a mechanic shop in the front and living space in the back. He went to a rent-to-own store and filled the house with new furniture, as if a new couch and bedroom set could create stability. I started another new school while still in first grade.

This time, though, I liked my school. It was a county school, and for a while I felt like I belonged. Our yard was big. Mandy and I ran freely and made friends quickly. I had learned by then how to adapt fast. Making friends was not optional when you moved constantly. It was survival.

For a short time, things felt manageable.

Then the drugs returned.

This time they changed him more dramatically. He began hallucinating. He would grab a knife and stab holes in the walls, convinced people were hiding behind them. He spoke to enemies that were not there. His mind seemed to turn against him, and we were caught in the aftermath.

At night, he made all of us sleep in their bedroom. The lights had to stay on. We were not allowed to cover ourselves with blankets. I never fully understood why. I only knew that he believed it was necessary. I lay awake staring at the ceiling, trying to make sense of a fear that was not mine but had become my burden.

The exhaustion followed me to school. I struggled to focus. I moved through the day in a haze. I told no one what was happening at home.

One night, his rage escalated again. He began knocking over furniture. Lamps shattered. Chairs fell. Even the refrigerator was pushed and rocked. Then he looked around at the destruction and told us to clean it up before he returned. Instead of walking out the front door, he climbed out the window and disappeared into the dark.

That was the environment we lived in. Chaos without warning. Fear without explanation.

In the middle of that instability, God sent a small but meaningful kindness. Our school bus driver was a gentle woman who also drove the church van. She invited Mandy and me to Sunday school. We started going regularly. Those mornings became the most peaceful part of my week. We memorized Bible verses, sang songs, and learned about a God who loved children. A God who protected. A God who saw.

That Christmas, the church filled our kitchen floor with gifts. Mandy jumped up and down shouting that she believed in Santa Claus. Her joy was pure and untouched by the weight we carried. For a few hours, we were just children opening presents instead of scanning rooms for danger.

But even that joy existed beside fear.

One night, I saw my mom fixing her hair and my dad getting dressed to leave again. I started crying and begged him not to go. I wrapped my arms around him and pleaded for him to stay home with us. He knelt down, wiped my tears, and turned on The Lion King before walking out the door.

Even my tears were not enough to make him stay.

That was the night something shifted inside me. I stopped expecting protection. I started assuming responsibility.

Not long after, I was called into the counselor's office at school. We were still living in Alabama, and someone had contacted Child Protective Services. I sat across from the counselor as she asked questions about being left home alone and about what life was like at home.

But I already knew what to say.

My dad had coached us carefully. If anyone asked, we were supposed to say they had gone to the grocery store. Nothing more.

So I lied.

I said they were only gone for a little while. I said everything was fine. I protected them the way I had been taught to.

That day could have changed everything. But the truth stayed hidden behind practiced words.

Looking back, I realize how unstable those years truly were. We moved repeatedly. I changed schools without warning. I learned to adapt before I learned to rest. Instability became normal.

And yet, even there, God was present.

He was present in the kindness of a bus driver. In Sunday school songs. In a Christmas morning filled with generosity. In the quiet strength forming inside me, even when I felt exhausted and afraid.

"The righteous cry out, and the Lord hears them; He delivers them from all their troubles." — Psalm 34:17

I did not always see Him clearly in those years. But He was building something in me that chaos could not destroy.

Even when I was left alone, I was never completely abandoned.

Chapter 5

Nowhere to Hide

After school ended at the close of my fourth-grade year, our time in Alabama came to an abrupt finish. Like so many moves before, it was not carefully planned. It was reactionary. We packed what we had and returned to my grandmother's house in Illinois. We were told it would only be temporary, just until my parents found another place to live. That promise had been repeated enough times that I no longer knew whether to believe it.

Before long, another house was found in Kentucky. Once again, we loaded everything into the car and started over. With every move, I tried to convince myself that this one would be different. Maybe a new town would reset something. Maybe a new job would stabilize my dad. Maybe this time we would stay long enough for life to feel normal.

But instability had become the pattern.

Before that school year even ended, my dad lost yet another job. The tension in the house returned quickly, heavy and suffocating. Soon we were packing again and heading back to Illinois. Each move felt less like opportunity and more like evidence that nothing in our lives could hold.

When we returned to my grandmother's house that time, something had shifted. My dad's drinking intensified, and his temper grew more volatile. The arguments between him and my mom escalated nightly. What had once been loud and chaotic became frighteningly deliberate. The yelling would begin, sharp and cutting, and then it would turn physical. I would lie on a pallet on the living room floor, pretending to be asleep while listening to the sounds of violence echo through the house. The thud of fists. My mother's cries. Objects crashing into walls.

I learned to stay still. I learned that movement could draw attention. I learned that silence felt safer than reaction.

Sometimes my grandmother would quietly gather us and take us to her antique store when the arguments became too intense. We would sit among old furniture and dusty shelves until things calmed down. Even then, the calm was temporary. We always went back. We always hoped the storm had passed.

But it had not.

The threats grew darker. My dad began saying he would kill my mom. At first, it sounded like anger speaking. Eventually, it sounded believable. One night he threw a butcher knife at her. Another night he chased her around the yard with the heavy metal hitch of a trailer, swinging it with full force. It crashed into the ground just seconds after she ran past. I remember realizing that survival had become a daily objective.

In his reckless anger, he would sometimes load all of us into the car and speed down gravel roads. The car would fishtail around curves, barely maintaining control. I gripped the seat and held my breath, wondering if this was the night we would not make it home.

In the middle of this chaos, my mom gave birth to her seventh and final child, a boy. After six daughters, my dad finally had the son he had always wanted. I hoped that would change something in him. I hoped it would soften the rage or shift his focus. It did not. If anything, his unpredictability intensified.

Then the violence turned toward me.

One night we were again sleeping on pallets in my grandmother's living room. I pretended to be asleep as usual, hoping to avoid attention. I felt him standing near me before I opened my eyes. Without warning, his steel-toe boot struck my side. The pain was sharp and immediate, but the physical pain was not what stayed with me. It was the realization. I had always believed that I was different, that my closeness to him protected me somehow. That illusion shattered in that moment.

There was nowhere to hide.

I understood then that loyalty did not guarantee safety.

Eventually, my mom left him. It was not dramatic. There was no frantic escape in the middle of the night. We left quietly while he was gone. We packed quickly and drove to Kentucky, where we entered a women's shelter. For the first time in years, the quiet felt different. It did not feel tense. It felt protective.

The shelter was small but structured. There were rules, schedules, and other women who carried their own stories of survival. I do not remember every detail of that summer, but I remember the counselor. She created a space where I could talk openly. One day she let me choose a stuffed animal from her office. I chose a tiger. It felt strong and fierce, and I wanted to feel that way too.

For a while, safety felt possible.

But even in the shelter, uncertainty lingered. I missed my dad. I missed the version of him I wanted to believe in. I believed he could change. I believed this separation might finally wake him up.

Looking back, I recognize how deeply I wanted to hold our family together, even at my own expense.

I do not know exactly what led my mom to return to him. Fear of raising seven children alone may have weighed heavily. Financial pressure was real. His promises likely sounded convincing. I also know that I told her I missed him. I know that I expressed hope that he could be different. I was still a child, still clinging to the idea that love could fix what addiction had broken.

So we left the shelter.

I held my tiger tightly as we packed, convincing myself that maybe this time the worst was behind us. I wanted to believe we were returning to something repaired.

But hope without change does not create safety.

And I was about to learn that lesson in a way I would never forget.

Chapter 6

The Night We Fled

It did not take long to realize that going back had not changed anything. If anything, my dad's anger felt more focused. It was no longer chaotic in the same way. It felt intentional, almost calculated. The first night we returned, he looked at my mom with a coldness I had never seen before. His voice was low, controlled, and filled with resentment. He asked her if she really believed she could leave and return without consequences.

Then he beat her.

I had seen violence before, but this felt different. It did not feel impulsive. It felt like punishment. I stood there frozen, watching blow after blow land, understanding something with painful clarity. The hope I had clung to during our time at the shelter shattered that night. I realized that love and loyalty were not enough to change someone who was not truly free from addiction and rage.

I knew then that if we stayed, something irreversible would eventually happen.

The night we fled is one I will never forget. My dad was passed out drunk on the couch, holding my baby brother in his arms. The house was quiet in a way that felt dangerous. My mom moved quickly but quietly, telling us to gather only what we could carry. There was no time for packing carefully. We slipped out to the van parked in the driveway, our hearts pounding.

She started the engine, drove across the road, and put the van in park. Then she turned around and told us to stay inside, not to move or make a sound. She had to go back for my brother.

Those minutes felt endless. We sat in silence, watching the house, waiting for the front door to burst open. I imagined headlights chasing us. I imagined him waking up and realizing we were gone. Every possible outcome raced through my mind. I wanted her to hurry, but I also understood that she could not leave my brother behind.

When she finally emerged from the side garage door with him in her arms, relief washed over me so strongly that I could barely breathe. She climbed into the driver's seat, her hands shaking as she closed the door. I helped buckle my brother into his car seat, and then she pressed the gas pedal.

We did not look back.

As we drove down that dark road, I kept waiting for headlights in the rearview mirror. I expected him to chase us. I expected chaos to follow. But the road remained empty.

We drove to Missouri, where my mom believed we would be safe. My dad would not think to look for us there. At first, we stayed in another shelter for battered women and children. The routine felt structured and protective. There were clear boundaries. There was supervision. There was safety in the predictability.

Eventually, my mom secured public housing, and I started sixth grade in yet another new school. For the first time in a long while, life began to feel stable. Mandy and I made friends quickly. Our home became a place where neighborhood kids gathered. We rode bikes around the block and laughed freely. I started to feel what it was like to exist without constant fear.

But trauma does not disappear simply because your location changes.

Over time, my mom began going out again. At first, it was occasional. Then it became routine. The bars that had once pulled my dad in began pulling her in as well. She hired an older teenage girl to babysit us, so we were no longer physically alone. On the surface, it appeared responsible. But something inside me felt uneasy.

One night, there was a knock at the door. I answered it. A man stood there asking for my mom. The moment I saw him, something in my body reacted. It was instinctive.

His presence felt wrong. I did not have language for it, but I trusted the feeling.

I told him he did not belong there and shut the door.

For a moment, I believed I had protected our home. But then my mom walked to the door and opened it. She let him inside.

The sense of safety I had begun to feel cracked. I could not stay in the house with him there. I walked out the back door and kept walking, not knowing where I was going. I only knew I needed distance.

As I moved down the street, I realized how fragile our stability had always been. We had escaped one form of danger, but new vulnerabilities were already forming. I was growing more aware. More protective. More distrustful.

The night we fled from my dad had felt like a clear line between danger and safety. But I was beginning to understand that safety is not just about geography. It is about boundaries. It is about protection. It is about adults who choose their children first.

And that was something I was still learning I could not control.

Chapter 7

Wanting to Be Wanted

I was thirteen.

Still a child, even though I did not feel like one.

By that age, I had already learned how to survive chaos. I knew how to read adults. I knew how to protect younger siblings. I knew how to stay quiet when things felt unsafe. What I did not know was how to understand my own worth. I carried unhealed wounds from years of instability, abandonment, and silence. I had learned that love could disappear without warning, and that being needed was sometimes confused with being valued.

At thirteen, attention felt powerful.

It started at a friend's house. I had spent time there before, and her home felt more stable than mine. But one night her older brother was having people over. The house was full of music, noise, and older boys. They did not look at me like a child. They looked at me like a girl.

That was new.

One of them paid special attention to me. He was older, confident, smooth in the way he talked. He leaned in close when he spoke, as if what I said mattered. For a girl who had grown up feeling invisible and displaced, that kind of attention felt intoxicating. It made me feel chosen.

When he asked me to go into another room with him, I went.

I did not fully understand what I was stepping into. I only understood that I wanted to feel wanted. I told myself it was harmless. Just a kiss. Just attention. Just proof that I mattered to someone.

But moments at thirteen can shape years that follow.

Word spread quickly. Suddenly, I was noticed. Boys called. They showed up. They sought me out. For a child who had spent years feeling unstable and overlooked, that attention felt like validation. I convinced myself it was love. I convinced myself it meant I had value.

But it was not love. It was desire without responsibility.

No one had taught me about boundaries. No one had explained how to guard my heart or protect my body. I had learned from a young age that compliance kept peace and silence prevented conflict. So when lines blurred, I did not push back. I did not say no. I did not even fully understand that I could.

Part of me believed that if I gave boys what they wanted, they would stay. That they would not leave like so many other people had. But they always left. And each time they did, the emptiness grew heavier.

I told myself I was in control. That I was making choices. But the truth is, I was thirteen and aching. I was trying to fill a space created by years of instability and unmet needs. I was searching for security in places that only offered temporary attention.

My mother must have noticed changes in me. The phone calls. The way boys began circling. The shifts in how I dressed and carried myself. But she never asked. She never warned me. She never said I deserved better. Her silence felt like permission, and I moved forward without guidance.

I began building walls around my heart. If I acted detached, I would not feel as disappointed. If I pretended not to care, maybe it would hurt less when someone disappeared. Outwardly, it looked like rebellion. Inwardly, it was grief and confusion.

Looking back, I see the connection clearly. A father whose presence was unpredictable. A childhood where I had to grow up too quickly. Early trauma that taught my body to freeze instead of resist. A deep fear of abandonment. All of it shaped the decisions I made at thirteen.

Rebellion was not the root. Woundedness was.

"The Lord is close to the brokenhearted and saves those who are crushed in spirit." — Psalm 34:18

At thirteen, I did not feel close to God. I felt embarrassed by my choices and unsure of who I was becoming. I believed that maybe I had already stepped too far outside of what was good. But now I understand something I could not see then. God did not look at me and see a rebellious teenager. He saw a wounded child searching for love in the only ways she understood.

Even when I ran toward the wrong things, He did not run from me.

Chapter 8

Betrayed and Broken

By the time we moved into my mother's new boyfriend's house in the country, I had learned to crave quiet. After years of chaos, yelling, and instability, silence felt like safety. The house was small but clean, tucked away from the noise of the city. There were no drunken fights shaking the walls. No furniture crashing to the floor. At first, it felt like a chance to breathe.

I wanted it to work.

But danger does not always announce itself loudly. Sometimes it enters gently, disguised as normal.

It began with marijuana. He offered it casually to Mandy and me, speaking as if it were harmless fun. I hesitated, but I saw my mom participate. If she was not concerned, I told myself I should not be either. The first time I smoked, the heaviness inside me softened. The constant edge of anxiety dulled. It felt like relief.

Then alcohol followed. The burn in my throat distracted me from the ache in my chest. Numbness became easier than awareness. I did not realize at the time that this was grooming. I only knew that I felt less burdened when I did not feel at all.

Then one night, the tone shifted.

He told me that if I wanted to smoke, I would have to get undressed.

At first I thought he was joking. I laughed nervously. But he was not laughing. The air in the room changed. My body reacted before my mind could process it. I froze.

I should have walked out. I should have said no. But when the adults in your life treat something as acceptable, especially when your own mother is present in the home, it becomes harder to trust your instincts. I had already learned that resisting adults often led to consequences. So I sat there, silent and shaking inside, trying to detach from what was happening.

The late nights became worse. Strip poker was introduced as a game. Every loss meant removing more clothing. Every round stripped away another layer of safety. I tried to sit out. I tried to avoid eye contact. But the pressure remained. I did not have the language then to name it as exploitation. I only knew something was deeply wrong.

One early morning, while I was staying at my cousin's house, the phone rang. Mandy's voice was barely steady.

She told me he had touched her. She told me she had fought him off.

The world stopped.

Anger rose in me with a force I had never experienced before. He had crossed a line with me, but now he had gone after my sister. My mom had been passed out in the next room. She had not heard anything.

I called her immediately and told her she had to leave. This time, she listened. We packed our belongings that same day and left his house.

Leaving did not erase what had happened. Mandy did not want to go to the police. She did not want to relive it. She did not want strangers asking her to explain something she barely understood herself. For a moment, it seemed like it might remain hidden.

Then we learned he had gone to my aunt and her husband and confessed. I do not know whether guilt drove him or fear, but he told them what he had done. My aunt and uncle chose to act. They went to the police.

The truth could no longer stay buried.

The investigation was exhausting. Sitting in a police station answering detailed questions forced me to relive moments I had tried to compartmentalize. They wanted timelines, descriptions, specifics. Some answers came quickly. Others felt like glass in my throat. Mandy was questioned as well. I saw the weight in her eyes, the strain of speaking about something that never should have been part of her story.

When the trial arrived, I felt both terrified and determined. Walking into the courtroom felt surreal. I saw him sitting there, expression blank. No visible remorse. No fear.

My aunts were present in the courtroom. Their faces were heavy with sorrow. Their presence mattered. For once, family members were witnessing the truth fully, not in whispers, not behind closed doors, but openly. I did not want them to hear the details. I did not want anyone to hear them. But silence had protected him long enough.

When I took the stand, my hands trembled. My voice felt unsteady at first, but I continued. I told the truth. I described what happened even when shame tried to crawl back into my chest. Abuse is cruel in the way it convinces victims that they are somehow responsible. I had to fight that lie as I spoke. I finished my testimony knowing I had done the hardest thing I could do.

Then we waited for sentencing.

I believed justice would feel solid and final. I believed that after everything Mandy endured, after the courage it took to fight him off and speak up, the system would respond with seriousness.

Instead, he received a short jail sentence and probation. That was all.

I remember feeling the air leave my lungs. After everything, the consequences felt small compared to the damage. I looked at the judge, hoping for more, hoping for something that matched the weight of what we carried. But the decision had already been made.

That day, I learned another painful truth. Betrayal does not only come from abusers. Sometimes it comes from systems that are supposed to protect.

I walked out of that courtroom feeling exposed and disappointed. I had expected justice to feel victorious. Instead, it felt incomplete.

"The Lord is a refuge for the oppressed, a stronghold in times of trouble." — Psalm 9:9

I wrestled with God in that season. I questioned why justice felt so partial. I wondered why protection had not come sooner. But over time, I began to understand that justice is not always fully realized in a courtroom.

Justice can also look like speaking.

Like refusing silence.

Like breaking cycles.

Like surviving.

We did not receive the sentence we believed was deserved. But we were not silenced. And survival, though not glamorous, is powerful.

God was present in Mandy's strength to fight back. He was present in my aunt's decision to report the truth. He was present when I took the stand. Even when the verdict disappointed us, He did not abandon us.

The system's justice felt incomplete. But God's justice is not finished.

Chapter 9

Back to Kentucky

Leaving the courthouse did not feel victorious. I had believed that telling the truth would bring closure, that speaking openly would somehow restore what had been stolen. Instead, I walked out feeling hollow. The verdict had been given, but it had not healed anything. Justice felt incomplete, and the emptiness inside me felt deeper than before.

Soon after, my mom was given the option to move back to Kentucky, closer to family. My aunt and uncle had spoken to the judge and case manager and offered a solution. If we moved into their rental house, they could help keep an eye on things and make sure we had support. On paper, it sounded stable. But I had lived long enough to know that plans and promises did not guarantee safety.

The house was small but decent. Another new school. Another new town. Another chance to try to blend in and pretend I was just like everyone else. I told myself I would keep my head down and stay quiet. I carried too much to ever feel normal. I walked the hallways aware of how different I felt inside, as if the weight of my past was something everyone else could somehow see.

For a short while, life appeared steady. Mandy and I spent time with our cousin, who had become our built-in best friend. Being around her felt familiar and grounding. But I did not fully relax. I had learned not to.

My mom's sister began coming around more often. She brought men with her. Strangers. They drank in the living room and laughed loudly, as if nothing in our past had taught us to be cautious. The house that was meant to represent oversight and stability slowly began to feel compromised. Mandy and I retreated to our room most nights, trying to make ourselves small. We listened to conversations we were not meant to hear. We smelled alcohol in the air. It felt like we had traded one form of chaos for another.

My uncle showed up one afternoon and confronted my mom. He reminded her that this was not what he had vouched for when he convinced the judge to allow us to move there. He had promised accountability and protection. I remember standing nearby, silently hoping she would defend us, that she would say she would fix it, that she would choose differently this time.

She did not.

She sat there in silence.

That silence settled heavily inside me. It confirmed something I had been afraid to fully admit. I was still waiting for her to become the mother we needed. And she still wasn't stepping into that role.

Then everything shifted again.

One afternoon, Mandy and I stepped off the school bus laughing about something small and ordinary. The moment I saw my grandmother's car parked outside the house, my stomach tightened. The house felt unnaturally quiet when we walked in.

My grandmother was sitting at the kitchen table. Her hands were folded, and her expression told me before she said anything that something was wrong. My mom was not there.

There was only a letter.

When I unfolded it, my hands were shaking. The words were short and almost detached. She wrote that she was not strong enough to take care of us. She said she could not do it anymore. She said she was leaving.

I stared at the page, waiting for something else. An explanation. An apology. A promise to come back. But there was nothing beyond those sentences.

She had walked away.

I did not cry at first. What rose up in me was not immediate sorrow but anger. A quiet, steady anger that settled deep in my chest. I was angry that she said she was not strong enough. I had been strong for years. I had fed babies in the middle of the night. I had stood between chaos and my siblings. I had sat in courtrooms and told the truth. I had survived things that should have crushed a child. And now my mother was telling us she could not.

I remember thinking, Then why did I have to be?

Why was I expected to carry so much when she could decide she was done?

That realization cut deeper than anything before it. My father's addiction had taken him from us piece by piece. But this felt like a choice. She was not forced out. She was not locked away. She chose to leave.

And she did not choose us.

That night, all seven of us were gathered in my grandmother's house, trying to fit our lives into a space that was never meant to hold that much hurt. I lay awake staring at the ceiling, feeling something shift inside me. It was not just sadness. It was the beginning of a belief that would follow me for years. If the people who are supposed to love you most can walk away, then love must not be secure. If your own mother can decide she is not strong enough, then you better learn to be stronger than everyone around you.

Abandonment rooted itself quietly that night. It whispered that I needed to take care of myself. It warned me not to depend on anyone. It convinced me that if I did not hold everything together, it would all fall apart.

I wanted to hate her, but anger and longing existed side by side. A part of me still hoped she would come back through the door and say she had made a mistake. She did not.

She was gone.

For the first time, I understood that some goodbyes do not come with screaming arguments or dramatic exits. Some come quietly, in the form of a letter left on a kitchen table.

In the stillness of that room, I asked God the same question I had asked so many times before. Why? Why did stability never last? Why did the people who were supposed to protect us keep leaving?

The answers did not come immediately. But one truth remained steady. Through prison sentences, courtrooms, shelters, and broken promises, God had not left.

"The Lord is close to the brokenhearted and saves those who are crushed in spirit." — Psalm 34:18

My mother had walked away. But my Father in heaven had not.

I did not understand how this would fit into a greater story. I did not see how any of it could be redeemed. But even in that moment of anger and grief, I sensed that my life was not over.

This was not the end.

Chapter 10

A Father's Return

Life had settled into a strange rhythm after my mom left. My grandmother drove Mandy and me from Illinois to Kentucky each day so we could stay in the same school. The drive was long, but it was consistent, and consistency felt steady. At the time, my dad was back in prison again, but we knew he would be getting out soon. His girlfriend had already come to stay at my grandmother's house to help with the younger kids, and we knew he would be coming there too once he was released.

It had been two years since I had seen him. During that time, he wrote to me often. His letters were filled with talk about God, about how prison had changed him, about how he wanted to do things right this time. He wrote about rebuilding our family and being present. The words sounded sincere. I wanted to believe them. After everything that had happened, I needed something to feel hopeful about.

The day he got out was Election Day in early November. I remember it clearly because it felt like a turning point. When I saw him again for the first time in two years, I felt relief. No matter what we had been through, he was still my dad. I had missed him.

That afternoon, he took me with him to the small grocery store nearby to pick up something for supper. It was a simple errand, but it felt meaningful. It was just the two of us in the car. No tension. No raised voices. Just conversation. I watched him carefully, noticing how healthy he looked. He always looked good when he first got out of prison. Clear eyes. Strong posture. Present. It made it easier to believe the change might be real.

At some point during the drive, he asked if I had been smoking cigarettes. I had been. With everything changing around me, smoking had become something that felt steady. It gave me something to do with my hands, something to focus on. I convinced myself it calmed me down. Whether it really did or not, I believed it helped.

When I admitted that I was smoking, he did not react with anger. Instead, he reached into his pack and handed me one.

"I don't want you overdoing it," he said, lighting his own. "But I'd rather you be honest with me."

I took it willingly. I wanted it. I wanted that moment. Sitting there beside him, sharing something simple, felt normal. It felt like connection. For a little while, it felt like maybe we could rebuild something.

The first few days after he came home were steady enough that I allowed myself to relax. I wanted so badly for this to work. I wanted one of my parents to stay solid. I wanted to stop waiting for the next collapse. His letters had promised change, and I held onto that promise tightly.

But as the days passed, I began to see familiar shifts in him. His thoughts became restless. His conversations jumped from one idea to another. There was a tension beneath the surface that I recognized. I did not say much about it. I just watched.

Thanksgiving arrived not long after. The house was full that morning. Pots clanged in the kitchen. Family members laughed. Kids ran in and out of rooms. For a few hours, it almost felt like a normal holiday.

He had been gone most of the day. When he finally walked through the door, I knew something was off. His movements were quick and unsettled. His eyes looked distant. He spoke about people watching him, about needing to stay alert.

Then he picked up a knife.

He held it firmly in one hand and reached for my hand with the other. His grip was tight, almost protective, as if he believed he was shielding me from a threat only he could see. In his mind, he was not the danger. He thought he was defending us.

My heart pounded, but I did not pull away. I had learned that panic only escalated situations. I squeezed his hand gently and spoke quietly.

"It's okay, Dad. We're safe."

I kept my voice steady and calm. I reminded him that there was no one there. That everything was fine. I stayed close to him until his breathing slowed and his shoulders lowered. Slowly, he set the knife down. He released my hand, and the moment passed as if it had never existed.

Only a few feet away, family members were still laughing over a card game, unaware of what had just unfolded in the kitchen. I stood there for a moment after he walked away, letting my body catch up with what had happened. Managing moments like that had become instinct. I did not think of it as bravery. It was simply survival.

The next day, he and his girlfriend left the house for a while. As soon as they were gone, I made a phone call to my mom's mom. My hands shook as I dialed. I did not want to create more chaos, but I also could not ignore what I had seen. My siblings deserved stability. They deserved safety.

I had wanted so badly for this reunion to work. I had believed his letters. I had believed in the possibility of change. But wanting something does not make it sustainable.

Soon after, arrangements were made. My aunts would take custody of us. The five oldest would go to Kentucky. The youngest two would go to Alabama. Hearing that felt like another fracture. We had already endured so much together. Now we were being divided.

Grief settled heavily in me. I was tired of rebuilding. Tired of adjusting. Tired of watching hope rise and fall. Each time I allowed myself to believe things might stabilize, something shifted again.

Yet through it all, one truth remained. Through prison sentences, abandonment, courtrooms, and broken promises, God had not left.

That night, through quiet tears, I whispered the only prayer I could manage.

"Lord, help me trust You in this."

Chapter 11

A New Home, A New Reality

Moving in with our aunt in Kentucky felt like another fresh start, though by then I had stopped counting how many fresh starts I had lived through. Every move carried a quiet hope that maybe this time would be different. Maybe this house would last. Maybe this version of normal would stick. But somewhere deep inside, I had learned not to expect permanence. Stability had always come with an expiration date.

Still, this transition felt different in one important way. This wasn't a shelter. It wasn't a stranger's house. It wasn't chaos disguised as opportunity. It was family. My aunt and uncle had always been involved in our lives, and they genuinely wanted to help. That mattered. Mandy and

I settled in carefully, aware of how much had already been done for us.

My cousin, who was our age, had grown up in a way that looked normal compared to our childhood. She had routine. Consistency. Security. But she never made us feel different. She did not treat us like we were broken or fragile. She treated us like we belonged. Over time, she became more than a cousin. She felt like a sister. Even though she had not lived through what we had, her presence lightened the weight we carried. Sometimes healing does not come through words or explanations. Sometimes it comes through laughter in a bedroom, shared secrets, and someone choosing to sit beside you without judgment.

For the first time in a long while, we experienced structure. There were rules. Expectations. Consequences. We ate meals together. We went to school consistently. We attended church every Sunday and Wednesday. Church had always been part of my life, but in that season it felt steadier. It was no longer just something I cried out to in the middle of chaos. It became something I stepped into intentionally.

That was the season Mandy and I made the decision to be baptized.

For years I had prayed out of desperation. I had begged God to fix things, to stop the fighting, to bring protection, to hold us together. But standing in that church, choosing baptism, felt different. It was not a reaction to crisis. It was a decision. A declaration that despite everything, I still believed. I still trusted Him.

When I stepped into the water, I did not feel fireworks or instant freedom. What I felt was surrender. I had carried pain for so long that I almost did not know who I was without it. Baptism did not erase my past. It did not undo trauma. But it marked something inside me. It said my story did not end with what had been done to me. It said I was choosing to walk forward with God, not just cry out to Him in emergencies.

For a while, life felt steady. There were small glimpses of normalcy I had never truly known before. I had a boyfriend from church, the kind of innocent teenage relationship that revolved around sitting together in youth group and passing notes during service. We would talk after church and laugh about small things. It was simple. It was safe. It gave me something light to hold onto.

There was also the boy next door. He had four-wheelers, and we would spend hours riding through the woods and along creeks. Mud would splash up our legs, and the wind would rush past my face. For those moments, I was not the girl with the complicated history. I was just a teenager laughing in the open air. I felt free in a way I had not felt before. Those afternoons were more healing than I realized at the time. They reminded me that joy was still possible. That my childhood had not been entirely stolen.

But even during the good moments, there was a quiet caution inside me. I had lived through too many "good seasons" to relax fully. I had learned that stability could shift without warning.

It was not easy for my aunt and uncle to suddenly take in so many children. They had opened their home out of love, but love does not erase exhaustion. I began to notice the strain in my aunt's eyes. The weariness in her voice. She was trying to manage schedules, emotions, trauma, and ordinary life all at once. She wanted to make it work. She truly did.

Eventually, the weight became too heavy.

One day she broke down.

I do not say that with judgment. I say it with understanding. Seven children, especially children carrying years of instability and hurt, was more than she had prepared for. She had given us structure and safety during a season when we desperately needed it. But she was human. And humans have limits.

When I realized another move was coming, something inside me did not panic the way it once would have. Instead, I felt tired. I finished out my eighth-grade year knowing that change was waiting again. Another goodbye. Another attempt at stability that I was not sure I believed would last.

This time we were moving to Alabama to live with my grandmother.

People called it a fresh start. I had heard that phrase too many times to let it mean much anymore. It did not feel fresh. It felt like another interruption. Another reminder that belonging had always been temporary.

I was tired of packing. Tired of adjusting. Tired of pretending that each move did not chip away at something inside me.

And yet, through every transition, one truth remained. God had been steady. When adults grew weary. When homes changed. When plans fell apart. He had not moved.

I did not know what Alabama would hold. I did not know if it would be calmer or harder. I only knew that wherever I went, He was already there.

And in a life where so much shifted, that was the only thing that did not.

Chapter 12

Running from the Pain

Moving back to Alabama did not feel like starting over. It felt like circling back to something unfinished.

By the time I packed my things again, I no longer argued with change. I no longer asked why. I folded my clothes, put them into boxes, and followed the next plan laid out in front of me. I had grown used to instability. It had shaped the rhythm of my life. But even though moving had become routine, something inside me was wearing thin. I was tired in a way that was hard to explain. Tired of adjusting. Tired of believing each new home might finally be permanent.

Living with my grandmother was familiar territory, but I was not the same girl who had lived there before. I was older now. More aware. I had seen how quickly adults could unravel, how easily hope could collapse. I had also begun to recognize my own limits.

At first, things seemed manageable. My grandmother had rules. She made sure we left for school in the mornings and expected us home in the afternoons. She did what she could. But she had already raised her children, and now she was raising us. There was only so much energy one person could give. Whether from exhaustion or trust, there were gaps in supervision. And Mandy and I slipped through them easily.

In the beginning, I tried to hold onto what I had found in Kentucky. One afternoon, I sat on the back porch steps with my dad and made him listen to a Third Day CD I had brought with me from my aunt's house. I held onto that CD like it was something solid. The lyrics felt grounding. They reminded me of who I had tried to be. I did not want to fall backward into the version of myself that chased escape. I wanted to believe that even if my surroundings changed again, I could stay steady.

But steadiness requires support, and I did not know how to create that on my own.

It started with our older cousin. She moved through life like nothing could touch her. Reckless. Confident. Unapologetic. She had already stepped into things I had only heard about. It did not take much for her to pull us in. She introduced us to pain pills and cough syrup, showing us how to use them in ways I had never imagined.

The first time the numbness settled over me, it felt like relief. Not excitement. Not rebellion. Relief. The constant ache inside me softened. The thoughts that normally circled my mind grew quieter. The disappointment, the abandonment, the exhaustion all faded into the background. For a little while, I did not feel heavy.

That feeling was enough.

By the time I started ninth grade, experimenting had turned into chasing. Mandy and I skipped school without much consequence. We learned how to leave in the morning and disappear until it was time to return. My grades stopped mattering. Planning for the future felt pointless when the present already felt unstable. The high was not about the pills themselves. It was about the silence they created inside me.

At home, everything appeared normal on the surface. My grandmother saw me leave and return. She saw a teenager coming and going. But she did not see what filled the hours in between. She did not see the nights we slipped out or the parties that formed when she went dancing on Fridays. The music would rise the moment her car pulled away. People we barely knew crowded into the house. Bottles passed from hand to hand. Laughter echoed through rooms that had once held bedtime prayers.

It looked like freedom. It felt like control. But it was neither.

This was not about having fun. It was about escape. I was trying to outrun the ache I carried from one house to the next. The ache of being left. The ache of never fully belonging. The ache of growing up too quickly and still feeling unseen.

The patterns returned easily. I did not know how to say no. Sometimes I did not even try. The pills dulled my body. The syrup slowed my thoughts. And the boys filled whatever space was left. I told myself I was choosing it. That I was in control. But deep down, I knew I was trying to prove something to myself. That I mattered. That someone wanted me.

Even if it was temporary. Even if it was shallow.

Afterward, guilt would rise up strong and sharp. I would hate myself for slipping again. But instead of stopping, I reached for the numbness harder. Because guilt was loud, and the high was quieter.

During this season, my dad drifted in and out of our lives. He had moved to Michigan with his girlfriend, but whenever their relationship fractured, he returned to Alabama looking for somewhere to land. One evening, he asked if I wanted to go for a drive. I agreed, thinking it was another attempt to bond, another chance for him to step into the role I still wished he could fill.

Not long into the drive, he asked if I wanted to drive. I was fifteen. No permit. No experience. But I nodded. I had never been good at telling him no.

We stopped at a gas station. He pumped the gas and got back in the passenger seat. When I hesitated, reminding him he had not paid, he told me to just go. My stomach tightened, but I drove away. I knew it was wrong. I knew it was reckless. But I also knew arguing would not change anything.

As the night went on, he drank heavily. His words blurred. Eventually, he climbed into the back of the van and passed out. Before he did, he said we were going to Michigan.

Twelve hours north.

I drove through the night with no heat, my feet numb, my hands stiff around the steering wheel. My only instruction had been to follow I-65 North. So I did. I tried not to think about how young I was. I tried not to imagine what would happen if I lost control of the vehicle. I tried not to panic.

When we ran low on gas, I woke him. He told me where to pull in. We filled up. Again, he told me to drive off without paying. Shame burned in my chest, but I obeyed.

When we finally reached Michigan, his girlfriend's son was standing outside waiting. He looked at us and said he had called the police. Before I could react, flashing lights filled the mirrors. My dad refused to get out of the van. The officers warned him. When he still did not comply, they maced the vehicle.

I will never forget the burn. The way it filled my lungs and eyes. I could not see. I could not breathe. I was pulled from the van and taken to the police station with him.

He was arrested.

I was left stranded in Michigan with his girlfriend until my grandmother drove all the way from Alabama to get me.

I had never felt more lost.

Looking back, I do not know how I survived that season. I could have wrecked that van. I could have been hurt at one of those parties. I could have spiraled further than I did. But I did not.

Because even in the middle of my running, God had not stepped away.

He was there on the porch when I played that Third Day CD, still reaching for Him in small ways.

He was there on that highway when I drove through the dark, terrified and numb.

He was there when the police lights flashed and everything spun out of control.

I was not seeking Him. Not fully. Facing Him would have meant facing myself. And I was not ready for that.

But He never left.

"You will seek me and find me when you seek me with all your heart." — Jeremiah 29:13

I had not reached that place yet. But even in my rebellion, He was already writing something I could not see.

Chapter 13

Left Behind, But Not Forgotten

After Michigan, everything felt fragile. My grandmother had done everything she could, but my dad's arrest was the breaking point. One evening I walked into her room and saw her sitting on the edge of her bed, phone pressed tightly to her ear, tears sliding down her face. I had never seen her look so defeated. She looked tired in a way that went deeper than sleep.

"They don't think I should be raising y'all anymore," she said softly.

I knew she loved us. That was never the question. But love does not refill an empty tank. She had carried us as long as she could.

Within days, Mandy and I were sent to our mom in Missouri.

From the moment we arrived, she told us the plan. Mandy and I were staying with her. The other three would be going to our aunt's house in Alabama, where our youngest two siblings already lived. She said it confidently, repeatedly, like she wanted it to sound solid.

And I wanted to believe her.

Even so, something inside me stayed guarded. I had heard promises before.

When it was time to leave Missouri, all five of us climbed into her boyfriend's single cab truck. There was no back seat. No extra space. Mom, Mandy, and I each held one of the younger kids on our laps for the entire five-hour drive to Alabama. It was cramped and uncomfortable, but that part didn't feel unusual. We were used to squeezing into whatever space life offered.

Somewhere along the dark highway, a cow stepped into the road. The truck hit it hard enough to knock out the headlight. The impact jolted through the cab and sent my heart racing. For a moment everything felt suspended.

Then we kept driving.

When we finally pulled into my aunt's driveway in Alabama, all five of us climbed out, stiff from the long ride. We grabbed our bags and walked toward the house. Our aunt wasn't home. Only her husband was there.

My mom said they needed to go into town to get the headlight fixed and that they would be back for us soon.

That was the moment it hit me.

Not loud. Not dramatic. Just a deep, sinking feeling in my stomach. It was the first time I can remember physically feeling sick from all the moving, all the shifting, all the instability. I felt depleted. Mentally done. I didn't argue. I didn't ask questions. But something inside me knew.

We carried our things inside.

They drove away.

I stood in the living room trying to quiet the nausea in my chest. I told myself not to assume anything. They would come back. That was the story.

But time stretched.

Eventually, my aunt's husband called Mandy and me into another room. He looked uncomfortable, like he wished he did not have to be the one to say it.

"She's not coming back," he said plainly. "This is where you're staying."

The hurt came first. That familiar ache that had followed me from house to house. Then anger rose up, steady and controlled. I was tired of being repositioned when life became inconvenient. Tired of being part of decisions no one explained.

But underneath both of those feelings was something colder.

Numbness.

I didn't cry immediately. I didn't scream. I just stood there, very still, feeling something inside me seal off. Earlier in my life, moments like this would have shattered me. This time, I felt myself harden instead.

It wasn't chaos separating us.

It was choice.

She had told us we were staying with her. She had repeated it enough that I almost trusted it. Deep down, I think I knew it wasn't solid. I just wanted it to be true.

That night, the weight of it pressed in on me. I went into the bathroom and opened the medicine cabinet. I wasn't trying to die. I was trying to quiet the noise inside my head. I swallowed Tylenol PM. NyQuil. Whatever I could find that promised sleep. I just wanted relief from the exhaustion and the anger that felt too heavy to carry.

I curled up in bed and whispered into the darkness, "How do I keep going, God?"

There was no dramatic answer. Just silence and my own breathing.

It was the second semester of ninth grade, and for once we stayed in the same school. Mandy and I walked the same halls. On the outside, it looked like stability. Inside, I felt displaced and worn thin.

My aunt ran her home with structure. Clear rules. Firm expectations. Church every time the doors were open. After a year of skipping school and chasing numbness, the boundaries felt suffocating. I thought she was trying to control me. I did not yet understand that boundaries can be protection.

Mandy struggled more openly. The rules pressed in on her in a way she could not tolerate. Eventually she was given the option to leave, and she chose to go. My aunt took her back to Missouri to our mom. From there, Mandy met an older man. He promised safety and affection but delivered control and abuse instead. She was fourteen.

Watching her leave felt like losing the one person who fully understood the life I had lived. We had survived everything side by side. Now we were walking different roads.

I stayed.

Part of it was exhaustion. Part of it was fear of more instability. But part of it was my younger siblings. I couldn't bear the thought of them feeling alone. If I couldn't fix our parents, maybe I could at least stay present.

The house wasn't soft. Discipline was firm and sometimes harsh. The younger ones often moved carefully, trying not to upset anything.

Her refusal to let our dad see us created more conflict. Angry voicemails filled with accusations came through. Other family members criticized her, saying she was overstepping. I felt pulled between loyalties I did not know how to untangle.

And yet, something quiet was happening underneath it all.

We were in church consistently. I joined youth group. I listened to messages about grace and redemption. I watched families worship together and wondered what it would feel like to belong to something steady.

Healing did not happen overnight. I still carried hurt. I still felt angry. I still wrestled with numbness. But beneath all of it, I sensed something steady.

God had not stepped away.

He was not forcing change. He was not demanding immediate trust. He was waiting. Patient. Present.

Waiting for me to believe that I was worth holding onto.

I had been moved from house to house. Passed from adult to adult. But I was not invisible.

Even when I felt displaced.

Even when I felt hardened.

Even when I felt forgotten.

God had not forgotten me.

Chapter 14

Searching for Love in the Wrong Places

Just when life started to feel structured again, something inside me began to unravel.

Youth group had become a safe space. I was learning about God's love, about grace, about purpose. For the first time, I was hearing that my past did not disqualify me, that my story was not over, and that God could still use someone like me. During worship, I felt something soften. I felt seen in a way that wasn't tied to performance or survival. There was healing beginning in me, even if it was slow.

But healing does not erase longing.

There was still a deep ache in me that church alone did not quiet. I wanted someone to choose me in a way that felt personal. Not spiritually. Not generically. I wanted someone to look at me and stay. After years of being moved from house to house and adjusted to fit other people's lives, I craved something steady and tangible. I wanted arms around me. I wanted reassurance I could hear out loud. I wanted to feel wanted.

Then he moved in.

He was older than me, confident in a way that made him seem grounded. He noticed me. He asked questions and actually listened to my answers. He made eye contact when he spoke, and after everything I had lived through, that kind of attention felt powerful. Mandy was gone by then, and the loneliness I carried had grown heavier. When he started talking to me more often, standing outside smoking cigarettes and inviting conversation, I found myself looking for reasons to be nearby.

At first, it felt innocent. Just talking. Just connection. But I began to anticipate our conversations. I felt disappointed on days when I didn't see him. Slowly, he became part of my routine, part of my emotional stability. He knew pieces of my story. He knew I had been through a lot. And instead of backing away, he leaned in. To me, that felt like love.

Somewhere along the way, I attached deeply. I told myself this was different from before. This wasn't reckless attention or numbing behavior. This felt intentional. I wasn't just trying to be wanted physically. I wanted to belong to someone. I wanted to feel anchored.

Without realizing it, I started placing my worth in his responses. If he texted quickly, I felt secure. If he seemed distant, my thoughts spiraled. If he complimented me, my entire mood shifted. I did not see at the time that I was asking him to fill wounds he had never created and could never heal.

I still went to church. I still raised my hands during worship and listened closely during sermons. But during the week, my heart was tangled up in him. I would hear truth spoken over me on Wednesday nights and then spend Thursday wondering why he hadn't reached out. It was a quiet tug-of-war inside me. God was drawing me toward something steady and lasting, but I was clinging to something immediate and visible.

For nine months, he became my world. I wrapped my identity around being his. I believed that this time love would not end the way it always had before. I convinced myself that being chosen by him meant I was finally enough.

Then he disappeared.

There was no dramatic ending. No clear conversation. Just distance and silence. One day he was present, and the next he was gone. No explanation. No goodbye.

The pain was different from the other losses in my life. This wasn't addiction pulling someone away. It wasn't chaos. It felt like rejection. I replayed every conversation in my mind, searching for what I might have done wrong. I wondered if I had needed too much or loved too deeply. I felt foolish for believing it would be different.

I stopped eating the way I should have. Sleep became restless. I moved through my days in a fog, trying to act normal while feeling hollow inside. I wasn't just grieving him. I was grieving what I thought he represented: security, someone choosing me, someone staying.

His leaving reinforced a fear that had followed me since childhood. People do not stay. If you love deeply, you will eventually be left.

And yet, in the middle of that heartbreak, the words I had been hearing at church began to surface in my mind. Scriptures I had memorized echoed back to me in the quiet.

"The Lord is close to the brokenhearted and saves those who are crushed in spirit." — Psalm 34:18

I did not fully believe it yet. I still thought love had to be earned. I still believed that if I gave enough of myself away, someone would finally keep me. But slowly, I began to see that the ache I carried was bigger than any boy could fill.

"I have loved you with an everlasting love; I have drawn you with unfailing kindness." — Jeremiah 31:3

God was not shaming me. He was not turning away because I had placed my heart in the wrong hands. He was patient. Even when I confused attention with love. Even when I chased what felt immediate instead of what was lasting.

For the first time, I began to recognize the pattern. I had been searching for love in places that could only offer temporary comfort. I wanted something human to fix something spiritual. I wanted someone visible to heal wounds that ran much deeper than I understood.

"I will lead her into the wilderness and speak tenderly to her." — Hosea 2:14

This heartbreak did not destroy me, but it exposed me. It showed me how deeply I feared being alone and how desperately I wanted to be chosen. And quietly, gently, God was teaching me that I already had been.

Chapter 15

Finding My Own Way

By the end of my eleventh-grade year, I was beginning to feel something I hadn't felt in a long time: joy. Not the kind that came from being noticed by someone or having a good day at school, but a deeper joy that settled quietly inside me. It was steady. Calm. The kind that whispered, you're going to be okay. For the first time in years, I could breathe without feeling like my past was sitting on my chest.

Life was not perfect. Healing didn't erase everything overnight. There were still triggers that caught me off guard, still days when shame tried to creep back in, still moments when loneliness made me question my worth. But those feelings didn't control me the way they once had. They no longer dictated my decisions. I was learning that my history did not have to determine my future.

I had a job. I had a car I was making payments on. I had responsibilities that belonged to me. That mattered. Every paycheck I earned, every mile I drove, every hard decision to do better felt like proof that I was capable. I wasn't just surviving chaos anymore. I was building something of my own. It wasn't glamorous, and it wasn't easy, but it was honest.

Healing showed up in ways I hadn't expected. It didn't arrive in one dramatic breakthrough. It came slowly, in small shifts. It was in the way certain memories didn't knock the wind out of me anymore. It was in the way I started smiling without forcing it. It was in learning to forgive myself for choices I made when I was hurting. I began to believe that God wasn't standing over me disappointed. He was walking beside me, steady and patient.

"Forget the former things; do not dwell on the past. See, I am doing a new thing." — Isaiah 43:18–19

I started to accept that the past was exactly that — the past. I couldn't rewrite it, but I could decide how it shaped me. Instead of letting it define me as broken, I began to let it refine me. I wasn't free from temptation or insecurity, but I was beginning to hope again.

And in that quiet season, something unexpected began to grow inside me.

I started praying differently.

Not desperate prayers. Not prayers rooted in fear of being alone. For the first time, I prayed for my future husband. I had never allowed myself to believe I deserved something stable, something God-centered, something lasting. But one night, lying in bed, I whispered a prayer asking God to prepare the man He had for me, and to prepare me for him.

That prayer became a habit.

I found an old notebook and began writing them down. Page after page, I poured out my hopes. I wrote about the kind of man I longed for — not perfect, not flashy, but steady. A man who loved God more than he loved attention. A man who would lead with humility, not control. A man who would value faithfulness over excitement. I prayed for his heart, his character, his protection. I prayed that wherever he was, God would be shaping him too.

As I wrote, something shifted in me.

For the first time, I wasn't trying to earn love. I wasn't chasing someone to fill the silence. I wasn't compromising to be chosen. I was preparing. I was trusting that I didn't have to settle. That I didn't have to give pieces of myself away just to avoid being alone.

"Take delight in the Lord, and He will give you the desires of your heart." — Psalm 37:4

I began to understand that delighting in the Lord didn't mean ignoring my desires. It meant surrendering them. Trusting that He knew what I needed better than I did. Instead of forcing relationships, I chose to focus on becoming healthy. I asked God to teach me patience. To grow my discernment. To help me recognize the difference between attention and love.

"The Lord is my portion," says my soul, "therefore I will hope in Him." — Lamentations 3:24

For the first time in years, I wasn't frantic. I wasn't trying to control outcomes. I wasn't clinging to whoever was nearby. I was resting in the belief that if God had someone for me, I didn't have to chase him down. I just had to grow.

"Therefore do not worry about tomorrow." — Matthew 6:34

Looking back, I can see how intentional that season was. God was not just healing my wounds. He was reshaping my expectations. He was teaching me that love should feel steady, not chaotic. Safe, not consuming. Anchored, not anxious.

I didn't know what was ahead. I didn't know when or how my prayers would be answered. But I knew something had changed inside me.

I was no longer searching for love in the wrong places.

I was learning to wait for it the right way.

Chapter 16

A Love I Had Prayed For

It was an ordinary evening. I was driving home from work, tired, music playing softly in the background, my mind somewhere between responsibility and rest. As I passed the park near our neighborhood, I glanced over and noticed my neighbor sitting in his car with his cousin. We had known each other in passing. A wave here and there. Nothing more.

A minute later, they pulled out behind me.

At first, I assumed it was coincidence. But then he sped up like he was about to pass me, only to slow down again. It was playful, unexpected, and it caught me off guard. I laughed out loud, something I hadn't done freely in a while. It was simple. Light. Harmless.

Curious, I turned onto a gravel road. They followed. We stepped out of our cars, and what started as teasing turned into conversation. The kind that doesn't feel forced. There was no pressure, no performance. Just two people talking under an open sky, learning each other in real time.

It felt easy.

I didn't realize then how rare that feeling was.

He wasn't flashy or overly smooth. He was steady. He listened when I talked. Not politely, but intentionally. He asked about my life and actually waited for the answers. And when I slowly shared parts of my story, he didn't flinch.

I did not enter that relationship as a whole, unscarred girl. I carried mistakes. I had been unfaithful in past relationships. I had made choices rooted in insecurity and fear of being left. I didn't understand healthy love. I understood survival. I understood clinging. I understood trying to secure affection before it disappeared.

But this felt different.

Not dramatic. Not chaotic. Just steady.

One afternoon, not long after we began spending more time together, I was at home cooking dinner for the kids when something broke on the ceiling fan. Panic set in immediately. I knew how tense the house could feel when something went wrong, and I didn't want to be the reason for another lecture or disappointment.

Without overthinking it, I called him.

He came over right away. No irritation. No questions about why I couldn't fix it myself. He just grabbed what he needed and handled it before my aunt and uncle came home. He didn't make a show of it. He didn't hold it over me. He simply showed up.

That mattered more than I knew how to explain at the time.

I wasn't falling in the reckless way I had before. I wasn't trying to secure him or perform for him. I was simply growing attached to someone who felt safe.

I had spent the previous year writing prayers in a notebook for my future husband. I had asked God for a man who loved Him, who would lead with gentleness and strength, who would be consistent. I had written those prayers quietly, not knowing when or how they would be answered.

And now I found myself sitting across from someone who carried the qualities I had written about.

Not perfectly. But genuinely.

My aunt began to notice how often we were together. Her tone shifted. Rules tightened. Curfews were emphasized. I understood some of her concern. I was still young. My track record with relationships wasn't exactly spotless. But inside me, something felt settled instead of frantic.

Two months before my eighteenth birthday, at the beginning of my senior year, I made a decision.

I moved in with him.

It wasn't a dramatic rebellion. It wasn't me running from structure. It was me choosing what felt stable. Maybe it was fast. Maybe it looked impulsive from the outside. But for the first time in my life, I felt like I was stepping toward something instead of scrambling away from something.

Then my birthday came.

We had been living together only a short time. That evening felt normal. Spaghetti for dinner. Conversation about our day. Nothing extravagant. I wasn't expecting anything more than time together.

When I walked into the bedroom, I saw a teddy bear sitting on the bed. In front of it was a small ring.

I turned around, and he was already kneeling.

There was no audience. No crowd. No production. Just him asking, quietly and sincerely, if I would marry him.

In that moment, my life didn't flash before my eyes. There wasn't dramatic music playing in my head. There was simply peace.

I said yes.

We were engaged for five months, but even that began to feel long to him. He started talking about how living together without being married didn't sit right in his spirit. He wanted to honor God. That conviction wasn't pressure. It was clarity.

So one day, without announcing it to anyone, we made a decision.

I checked out of high school for the day. Called in to work. We drove to the courthouse together.

It was simple. No dress. No guests. No ceremony. Just paperwork and promises.

And in the middle of that ordinary day, something unexpected happened. His brother's mom happened to be at the courthouse getting a car tag. When she saw us, she lit up with excitement and insisted on documenting it. She ran to grab a disposable camera and came back to take pictures of us signing papers and smiling nervously.

I am still grateful she did.

There was no aisle. No flowers. No crowd clapping.

Just two young people choosing each other.

Looking back now, I can see the thread that ran through it all. The nights I wrote prayers in that notebook. The season of learning to wait. The shift from chasing attention to asking God for something steady.

He did not erase my past. Marriage did not magically heal every wound. We were young. We had growing up to do. There were challenges ahead we could not yet imagine.

But in that season, I felt something I had not felt before.

Chosen.

Not for what I could offer. Not because I was convenient. Not because someone needed to be saved.

Chosen.

"I have found the one whom my soul loves." — Song of Solomon 3:4

For the first time in my life, love did not feel chaotic.

It felt like peace.

Chapter 17

A Grief I Never Expected

For the first time in my life, I was genuinely happy. We had only been married a few months. It was January, a new year, a new name, a new beginning. Life felt steady in a way I had never experienced before. I had a husband who loved me, a home that felt safe, and a quiet peace settling into the places that had once felt chaotic. I wasn't bracing for the next crisis. I wasn't waiting for something to fall apart. I was finally exhaling.

Then April came.

The knock at the door wasn't loud, but it felt heavy. When I opened it and saw my aunt's husband standing there, I knew something was wrong. His face told me before his words did. There are moments in life when your body recognizes the weight of news before your mind can form the thought. This was one of them.

"Your dad has been murdered."

The sentence didn't feel real. It hung in the air between us, and for a second I expected it to rearrange itself into something else. But it didn't. Blunt force trauma to the head. A fisherman had found his body in the river. He had been there for three weeks.

Three weeks.

No one had reported him missing. He had been living alone. Quiet. Disconnected. The kind of absence that doesn't raise alarms.

My body reacted before my heart could process it. My chest tightened, my vision blurred, and I rushed to the bathroom. I barely made it before I got sick. Shock has a way of moving through you physically before you can form a coherent thought. I remember sitting on the cold tile floor, my hands shaking, trying to steady my breathing.

The kids were spending the night with me. I couldn't fall apart in front of them. I didn't even know how to fall apart for myself.

I called my husband. I don't remember exactly what I said, only that my words came out broken and rushed. He didn't ask questions. He didn't hesitate.

"I'm coming home," he said.

As I waited for him, memories flooded in without permission. Six months earlier, I had picked my dad up from a hotel he was staying in. We spent the day driving around, listening to music, laughing in a way we rarely did.

It wasn't dramatic. It wasn't life-changing. But it was light. Easy. One of the rare days when addiction didn't seem to be steering the wheel. I didn't know at the time that it would be one of our last good memories.

Our final phone call had been two months before he died. We talked about normal things. I was too afraid to tell him I had gotten married. I knew he wouldn't react badly, but I also knew it would stir something in him. He had always carried complicated feelings about the men in my life. He knew we were living together, but marriage felt different. Bigger. I told myself I would tell him soon.

Soon never came.

For most of my life, I had learned to guard myself from him. I loved my dad, but I also feared the instability that followed him. Addiction made him unpredictable. Sometimes tender and reflective. Other times distant and unreachable. I had built boundaries to survive him. I had prepared myself for disappointment. But I had never prepared myself for this.

What surprised me most was not just the sadness. It was the finality.

Somewhere deep inside me, I had always held onto a quiet hope that he would fully change. That one day he would stay sober. That he would settle into the faith he always talked about when he was in prison. That he would become the steady father I needed him to be. I knew he loved Jesus. I believe that with everything in me. But the pull of addiction was a shadow he never fully escaped.

With his death, that hope died too.

There would be no late-life redemption story. No restored years. No moment where everything circled back and made sense. There would be no version of him growing old and stable, calling to check on his grandkids. That future was gone.

And I had to grieve not only the father I had, but the father I wished I'd had.

"My flesh and my heart may fail, but God is the strength of my heart and my portion forever." — Psalm 73:26

Grief like that is complicated. It isn't clean. It doesn't sit politely in one emotion. I felt sorrow. I felt anger. I felt regret for things unsaid. I felt relief that the chaos was over. And then I felt guilty for feeling relief. It was a storm of contradictions.

The next morning, we told the kids. I watched their faces as they tried to understand what death meant in this context. Some of them had good memories. Some had confusing ones. I wanted to protect them from the weight of it, but I couldn't. So I gave them what little certainty I had left. God was still with us. Even here.

"The Lord is close to the brokenhearted and saves those who are crushed in spirit." — Psalm 34:18

Waiting for official identification felt endless. Even though we knew, a small part of us held onto the possibility of a mistake. When the dental records confirmed it, that fragile hope disappeared. This was real. There was no undoing it.

Although he had died in Kentucky, we arranged for him to be buried in Tennessee beside his father. That detail mattered to me. It felt like returning him to something familiar, something rooted.

The funeral was simple. A graveside service. No open casket. His body had been in the river too long. In some strange way, that felt merciful. I didn't have to reconcile the image of him in that condition with the man I remembered.

My aunt and uncle brought their guitars and sang. Their voices carried across the cemetery air, steady and soft. Family members spoke. A pastor talked about mercy and eternity. My mom was there. Mandy was there. For that brief window of time, all the fractures in our family paused. We stood shoulder to shoulder, bound not by history, but by loss.

As we looked down at the fresh earth, the reality settled in.

He was gone.

Not just distant. Not just unreachable. Gone.

And yet, even in that moment, I felt something steady beneath the grief. I wasn't standing alone. I wasn't carrying this in my own strength. God had walked me through chaos, abandonment, addiction, and fear. He was not going to leave me here in the aftermath.

I had lost my father.

But I was not fatherless.

And even in the grief I never expected, God was still holding me.

Chapter 18

A Love Too Strong to Ignore

Life at my aunt's house had grown tense long before anyone said it out loud. I could hear it in my siblings' voices when they managed to call me in secret. My aunt had forbidden them from reaching out, but kids find ways when they're desperate. They didn't always tell me details. They didn't have to. The hesitation in their voices, the way they tried to sound normal when they weren't, told me enough.

Something wasn't right.

Then one evening, her husband called me. His tone was measured, almost careful.

"She's talking about splitting them up," he said.

The words hit me like a physical blow. Splitting them up. As if they were objects that could be rearranged to make life easier. They had already lost parents in every way that mattered. They had already moved more times than children should have to count. The thought of them being separated from each other felt unbearable.

I had just started building my own life. I was newly married. I was about to graduate high school. I was supposed to be thinking about adulthood in slow, manageable steps. Instead, I felt the weight of five lives pressing against my chest.

They weren't just my siblings. They were pieces of me. I had changed diapers. I had braided hair. I had sat with them through nightmares. Loving them wasn't optional. It was instinct.

My husband and I sat down with his grandparents, who lived across the street from my aunt. They had seen the tension. They knew things weren't stable.

"They'd be better off with you," his grandmother said quietly. "Even at your age, I know you'll do right by them."

Her words steadied me and terrified me at the same time. I was eighteen. The world would have called me unqualified. But the truth was, I had been stepping into responsibility my entire life. Age did not determine readiness. Love did.

Still, I was scared. Not just of failing them, but of what it would cost. What would it do to our marriage? To our finances? To the small dreams we had barely begun to dream?

When my mom came into town for my graduation, I told her what was happening. To my surprise, she immediately began gathering paperwork for temporary custody. Watching her sign documents felt surreal. For so long, she had struggled to care for us. Now she was legally handing that role to me.

I tried speaking with my aunt before anything became official. I wasn't attacking her. I knew she was overwhelmed. But I couldn't ignore what the kids were telling me.

"You're too young for this," she said sharply. "You need to live your lives. I'm just working too much. It's a lot."

Maybe it was. But it was more than that. The house didn't feel safe. It didn't feel steady. And the kids needed more than someone barely holding it together.

Graduation day arrived. I wore my cap and gown. I smiled for pictures. I shook hands. But inside, I wasn't thinking about college or career paths. I was calculating grocery bills and bedroom space. I was wondering how to turn love into something practical.

That night, my siblings stayed with us. With Mom in town, it almost felt normal. Almost.

The next morning, we told my aunt our decision.

My stomach was in knots. I expected yelling. Resistance. Accusations. Instead, she was quiet for a long moment.

"If it was your mom, I'd fight it," she said finally. "But since it's you, I won't."

It wasn't approval. It was surrender.

Within hours, she began bringing over their belongings. Trash bags filled with clothes. School backpacks. Toys. Little pieces of their lives. Each trip from her house to ours made it more real.

They were ours now.

And we were barely adults.

At the time, we lived in one room in a house shared with my father-in-law. One bunk bed. Five kids. Two newlyweds. No savings to speak of. No blueprint.

I lay awake that first night staring at the ceiling, listening to the sound of breathing layered across the room. I wasn't afraid of loving them. I was afraid of not being enough.

We needed space. Quickly.

After weeks of searching, we found a used double-wide trailer already set up on a small piece of land. Ironically, it was right next door to my aunt. Three bedrooms. Two bathrooms. Nothing fancy. But it was ours.

We filled it with what we could afford, which wasn't much. Yard sale couches. Donated tables. Mismatched dishes. It didn't look like the homes in magazines. But it held laughter. It held arguments and apologies. It held healing.

At the time, I was working long hours at a nail salon, sometimes ten hours a day, six days a week. I would come home exhausted, barely able to think straight. My husband stepped into a role most young men would have run from.

He drove them to practices. Helped with homework. Showed up to games. Cooked when I couldn't.

I watched him carefully in those months. I worried about what this had cost him. This was not the life most nineteen-year-old boys imagined. Sometimes we would lie in bed in silence, both too tired to speak, both wondering if we had taken on more than we could handle.

We never said it out loud, but the question hovered between us.

Are we going to survive this?

There were moments I grieved the life we skipped. We never had the carefree newlywed season. There was no quiet house. No spontaneous trips. No nursery decorated just for our own baby. Sometimes I mourned what could have been. Not because I regretted them, but because I was human.

And then I would hear them laughing in the next room.

I would see one of them sleeping peacefully, no longer bracing for chaos.

And I knew.

This was hard. But it was right.

As the years passed, the dynamic shifted. The two oldest eventually left around fifteen. That loss cut deeper than I expected. I had poured everything I had into protecting them, guiding them, loving them. When they chose different paths, I questioned myself.

Had I failed?

But I learned something painful in that season. Love cannot control outcomes. It can only create a foundation.

Even then, I trusted God with what I could not fix. I had spent my childhood wishing someone would choose me. Now I was choosing them.

Raising my siblings was not part of any plan I had imagined. It cost us financially. Emotionally. Physically. There were seasons when I felt resentment flicker at the edges of my exhaustion. There were seasons when my body began to wear down from the constant responsibility.

But there was also grace.

Grace that carried us through grocery lines when money was tight. Grace that held our marriage steady when stress tried to fracture it. Grace that reminded me that sacrificial love is rarely glamorous, but it is always powerful.

We were young. We were imperfect. But we were committed.

And sometimes love is not loud or dramatic.

Sometimes it is simply refusing to let go.

Chapter 19

Miracles and Heartaches

After everything we had already carried in life, I assumed having children would come easily. I had always pictured motherhood unfolding naturally, almost gently. But month after month passed with nothing but negative pregnancy tests and quiet disappointment. At first, I told myself to be patient. We were young. There was time. But as the months stretched on, doubt crept in. I had taken on so much responsibility so early in life that a quiet fear began whispering that maybe this, too, would be complicated.

When I was diagnosed with polycystic ovarian syndrome, the relief of having an answer was quickly followed by grief. PCOS meant this might not be simple. We began fertility treatments with cautious hope. Each month followed the same cycle: anticipation, prayer, and then heartbreak. Over time, the disappointment touched more than my expectations. It touched my confidence. I questioned my body. I questioned whether something in me was broken.

One night, after another negative test, I sat on the bathroom floor long after I needed to. I whispered, through tears, "Lord, if this isn't Your will, take the desire away." But the desire never left. Eventually, what shifted was not my longing but my grip on it. I told God I would trust Him, even if motherhood looked different than I imagined.

Not long after that surrender, I conceived naturally.

I remember staring at the positive test, afraid to celebrate too quickly. During my pregnancy, I had a vivid dream of a baby girl with dark hair curled against my chest. When she was born and would only sleep resting on me, it felt like a quiet confirmation that God had not overlooked my tears.

Three weeks later, fear interrupted our joy.

We were visiting my grandmother when she touched the baby's forehead and said she felt warm. Something in me tightened. When I checked her temperature and saw 103 degrees, panic set in. At the pediatrician's office, everything moved quickly. Tests were ordered. A catheter. A spinal tap. I stood there watching nurses work on my tiny baby while I tried to steady myself. She was diagnosed with a severe kidney infection and admitted immediately.

Weeks later, specialists confirmed she had grade 5 kidney reflux, the most severe form. Infection after infection followed. I learned to live in a constant state of watchfulness. I learned the difference between a tired cry and a pain cry. When she was fifteen months old, doctors told us surgery was unavoidable. Handing her over that morning felt like surrendering something far too precious. When the surgeon finally told us the procedure had gone well, relief flooded me so intensely I could barely stand. Slowly, her health improved. The infections stopped. Her laughter returned.

Then life kept moving.

I became pregnant again. Then again. Over five years, I gave birth to four children. Our home grew louder, fuller, busier. There were diapers stacked high, laundry that never ended, nights that blurred into mornings. It was exhausting, but it was beautiful.

At the same time, we were still raising my younger siblings.

As the years passed, the weight inside our home began to shift. We were young. We were determined to build something stable and different from what we had known. We wanted order. We wanted safety. And sometimes our desire for stability turned into rigidity. We enforced rules tightly, sometimes too tightly. We were afraid of things unraveling, afraid of watching history repeat itself. When boundaries were pushed, we reacted quickly and at times harshly.

Looking back, I can see how overwhelmed we were. We were parenting from exhaustion. We were still growing ourselves while trying to guide them. There were days when our patience ran thin. Moments when discipline came from fear more than wisdom. We were doing the best we knew how, but we did not always get it right.

The two oldest felt that tension deeply. By fifteen, they were pushing against the structure we had built. What felt like protection to me may have felt suffocating to them. When the first one left, it broke me. I replayed conversations in my mind, wondering if I had been too strict, too sharp, too unbending. I questioned whether I had loved her well enough or simply tried too hard to control what I feared losing.

When the second left not long after, the grief settled heavier. I learned in that season that love does not guarantee outcomes. We had provided stability and sacrifice, but we were also young and imperfect. I carried regret, but I also carried compassion for the young woman I was—trying to hold together more than most eighteen-year-olds ever should.

At the same time, after my third child was born, something inside me shifted in a different way. What I first labeled as exhaustion revealed itself as postpartum depression. I loved my children fiercely, but I felt disconnected from myself. I cried without knowing why. I moved through my days in a fog. Gratitude and heaviness existed side by side. I felt guilty for struggling in a season I had prayed so hard for.

Healing did not come dramatically. It came slowly. Through quiet prayer. Through opening Scripture even when I felt numb. Through showing up for my children even when my emotions lagged behind. Over time, the fog began to lift. I found myself laughing again, present again.

Eventually, I became a stay-at-home mom, and the youngest three siblings were finishing high school. That season felt different. The house no longer felt like it was bracing for crisis. There was still noise, still chaos, still mess—but underneath it was steadiness. I was not just responsible for their survival anymore. I was able to enjoy them. We sat longer at the table. We laughed more freely. I saw resilience forming in them.

Watching the younger three graduate and step into adulthood felt whole in a way the earlier departures had not. It was bittersweet, but it was peaceful. I had helped raise them through critical years. I had done what I could.

When I look back on that season, I see miracles and heartaches woven tightly together. Infertility and answered prayer. Surgery and healing. Children born and children walking away. Discipline and regret. Exhaustion and restoration.

None of it was simple.

But through every high and every breaking point, God was steady.

MISTY FIELDS

I did not always have clarity. I did not always have strength. But I was never alone in carrying it.

"The Lord will fight for you; you need only to be still."
— Exodus 14:14

Chapter 20

A Love Worth Celebrating

I had been married for ten years, but I had never had a real wedding.

There had been no white dress, no aisle, no moment standing before family and friends to speak vows out loud. When we first married, none of that seemed important. We were young. We were building a life from scratch. Survival and responsibility had taken priority over celebration. Our vows had been spoken in a courthouse and then lived out quietly in the trenches of everyday life.

Marriage, for us, was never about the event. It was about showing up. It was about late nights with sick babies, early mornings filled with responsibility, and choosing each other when we were too tired to be romantic. We made promises in grocery store aisles, in whispered prayers, in moments when one of us felt like giving up. That had always been enough.

But as the years passed, I realized something inside me longed for more than endurance. I wanted a moment to pause. To look at what we had built and acknowledge it. Not because I needed a stage or attention, but because I wanted to honor the journey.

My husband saw that before I ever said it out loud.

On our anniversary, he took me to dinner. It felt simple and unassuming, just the two of us stealing a quiet evening. Afterward, as the sun dipped low and the sky turned gold, he stopped near the river, reached for my hand, and dropped to one knee.

He asked me to marry him again.

I laughed before I cried. Of course I said yes. But this time the yes felt layered. It wasn't the excitement of a young girl starting something new. It was the steady agreement of a woman who knew the cost of commitment and had already paid it.

That proposal carried the weight of everything we had survived together. Grief. Financial strain. Postpartum depression. Raising siblings while raising babies. Nights where we felt more like teammates in crisis than newlyweds in love. And yet, through all of it, we had chosen each other.

We decided to renew our vows that summer.

This time, I would have a dress. This time, we would stand before God and speak aloud what we had already proven in action. I began looking for a gown that felt like me, not like the eighteen-year-old bride I once would have been, but like the woman I had become.

When I found it, I knew. It wasn't about lace or fabric. It symbolized restoration. It represented the years that had shaped me, the scars and strength both.

My siblings and my mother-in-law were part of the process. They came with me to look at dresses, laughed during alterations, and shared in the anticipation. It meant more than they probably realized. They had witnessed the hard seasons. Now they were celebrating the fruit of perseverance.

Life did not pause for wedding planning. One of my siblings graduated just before the ceremony, another reminder of how much time had passed since we first said "I do" in that courthouse. We had grown up while building a family. We had skipped certain milestones and carried others early. This celebration felt like reclaiming something without erasing the years that came before it.

When the day finally arrived, it felt surreal.

The ceremony was held in our church, the same place where we had worshiped through heartbreak, prayed through exhaustion, and leaned on God in seasons when we felt empty. Standing there in that sanctuary felt right. This was where our faith had deepened. This was where we had been held up when we could not hold ourselves steady.

In the dressing room, I studied my reflection. I did not see a young bride filled with naïve expectations. I saw a woman who had been stretched, refined, and strengthened.

I saw a mother. A sister. A wife who understood that love is not sustained by emotion alone but by daily choice.

When the music began and I stepped into the aisle, I locked eyes with my husband. In his expression, I saw every chapter we had lived. The quiet strength he carried when I fell apart. The patience he showed when our home felt overwhelming. The prayers he whispered when we did not know what to do next.

We spoke our vows slowly, deliberately. Every word carried history. We were not promising something untested. We were reaffirming something proven.

After the ceremony, the church filled with laughter and celebration. Our children ran through the room, unaware of how sacred the moment was. To them, it was simply a party. To me, it was evidence. Evidence that love, when anchored in faith and commitment, endures.

One of the most meaningful moments of the evening was dancing with my baby brother. Years earlier, I had stood in a different role in his life, more caretaker than sister. That dance felt full-circle. We had both survived chapters that could have broken us. Now we were standing in a different season.

There is one photograph from that day I treasure most. I am standing in my gown, surrounded by our four children. My youngest, only six months old, is sitting on the train of my dress. It captures everything we had built. Not a flawless life, but a faithful one. Not easy, but intentional.

That night, we packed the car and drove to the beach with the kids. There was no elaborate honeymoon. Just the six of us walking along the shoreline, waves brushing against our feet. The wind carried salt and quiet reflection.

As I stood there watching my children run ahead and my husband walking beside me, I felt something settle deep inside.

This was the life I had prayed for.

Not a life without hardship. Not a life untouched by grief. But a life where love endured. A life where faith had carried us through every fire.

Marriage, I learned, is not defined by a wedding. It is defined by staying. By forgiving. By choosing each other again and again when circumstances test you. It is built in kitchens, hospitals, living rooms, and prayer closets long before it is celebrated in a sanctuary.

That day was not about rewriting our story.

It was about honoring it.

And it was a love worth celebrating.

Chapter 21

Faith, Family, and a Business Built on Prayer

That fall, one of my sisters came to us with life-changing news. She was pregnant.

She had only graduated high school a few months earlier. She was young, and even though she had her own apartment and a steady job, I could see the fear behind her brave face. She wasn't careless or irresponsible. In fact, she had already been standing on her own two feet in a way many people her age hadn't. But becoming a mother changes everything, and she knew it.

Even in her uncertainty, there was a quiet strength about her. She was determined to do whatever it took for her baby. Watching her step into that responsibility with seriousness and resolve made me proud. She wasn't running. She was rising.

A couple of months into her pregnancy, everything shifted. She began having complications, and her doctor referred her to a specialist in a larger city. I went with her. I needed to be there.

We sat in that cold exam room, the air thick with anxiety. The doctor spoke carefully, but his words landed like a blow to the chest. Her amniotic fluid was leaking. There was very little left protecting the baby. He told us the baby had only a five percent chance of survival. Even if she carried him to delivery, his lungs likely wouldn't develop fully. If he was born alive, he might only live for a few hours.

Five percent.

It is a strange thing to hear statistics about a child who already has a name in your heart.

I watched my sister absorb the news. I expected panic. I expected collapse. Instead, she chose courage. Without hesitation, she decided she would carry him for as long as she could. No matter what.

She was admitted to the hospital and placed on strict bed rest. From that moment on, our lives revolved around waiting and praying. I drove back and forth as often as I could, sitting beside her hospital bed, trying to keep her spirits steady while fighting my own fear.

At night, when the house was quiet, doubt would creep in. The doctor's words replayed in my mind. One night, overwhelmed and exhausted, I fell to my knees beside my bed. I cried out to God and confessed the fear I was carrying. I asked Him to forgive my doubt. I begged

Him to spare that tiny life and to give my sister strength for whatever lay ahead.

She spent six long weeks in that hospital room. Six weeks of monitors, uncertainty, and faith stretched thin. Then, at only twenty-eight weeks, she went into labor.

He was born weighing just two pounds and five ounces.

He was impossibly small, fragile in a way that makes your heart ache just to look at him. But he was breathing. Against all odds, he was alive.

He spent the next three months in the NICU, surrounded by machines and wires, fighting for every ounce he gained. When he finally came home, he was still on oxygen. Every breath felt like a miracle. Watching my sister walk through that storm with unshakable determination deepened my own faith in ways I cannot fully explain. The doctors had given him five percent. God gave him life.

Just days before we found out she would be placed on bed rest, I had signed a lease to open my own nail salon.

It should have been one of the most exciting moments of my life. I had prayed over that decision for months. I had dreamed of building something of my own, something that allowed me to provide for my family while still being present. But suddenly, the timing felt overwhelming. I was launching a business from scratch while driving back and forth to the hospital, juggling motherhood, marriage, and responsibility on every side.

I wanted to be in that hospital room more than I was. Every time I left her, it felt wrong. But life did not pause. My children still needed me. Bills still needed to be paid. The lease was signed.

When I finally opened the doors to the salon, the first few months were painfully slow. There were days I sat in that quiet space alone, the hum of the lights louder than any customer conversation. Doubt whispered constantly. What if I had made a mistake? What if I had stepped out too soon?

One afternoon, sitting at my nail table with no appointments booked, I pulled out a notebook and began writing prayers. I prayed over that shop the way I had prayed over my sister's baby. I asked God to build it if it was meant to stand. I asked Him to send the right clients, to make it sustainable, to let it bless my family instead of burden it.

The salon was only two minutes from the kids' school and daycare. That detail mattered to me more than square footage or decor. I refused to go back to the exhausting schedule I had worked before. If this business was going to succeed, it had to support my calling as a mother, not compete with it.

Slowly, things began to shift. One client turned into two. Two turned into a steady rhythm. Word of mouth spread. Women came not only for nails but for conversation, for encouragement, for a safe place to exhale. Before long, the shop felt less like a business and more like an extension of my living room. There were tears shared across that table. Prayers whispered quietly. Laughter that filled the space.

Eventually, one of my sisters joined me from another salon. It was a risk for both of us, but we stepped into it together. What began as a small leap of faith grew into something steady and strong. That business was built on more than skill. It was built on prayer.

Life in that season felt full in a way I had never experienced before. Three months after my sister brought her miracle baby home, another sister got married.

The most powerful moment of that wedding was not the dress or the flowers. It was watching my husband walk her down the aisle.

Our father was not there. But she was not alone.

My husband stepped into that role without hesitation. He walked beside her with quiet strength, giving her away with the kind of dignity and protection every daughter deserves. As I watched them, emotion rose in my throat. God had provided a covering for my sisters in ways we never could have predicted.

About a year later, another sister married on the beach. Once again, my husband walked her down the sand, waves rolling beside them. Before she said her vows, he prayed over her and her future husband. It was tender and powerful all at once. Standing there, I felt the ache of what we had lost in our father, but I also felt overwhelming gratitude for what God had provided instead.

In the middle of miracles, business growth, weddings, and babies, I could see something clearly: God had been weaving restoration into every broken thread of our story.

The little girl who once feared instability was now standing in a season of faith, family, and provision. Not because life had become perfect, but because God had proven Himself steady.

And in that steadiness, I found peace.

Chapter 22

Healing, Home, and the Journey in Between

About a year after opening my salon, something unexpected began to rise to the surface. It wasn't a crisis. It wasn't an event anyone else could point to. It was internal. Quiet. But persistent.

For years, I had survived by staying busy. Raising children. Running a business. Supporting siblings. Managing a household. There was always something that needed me. And as long as I was needed, I didn't have to sit still long enough to feel what I had buried. But when life finally steadied, the silence gave space for old wounds to breathe.

At first it showed up as heaviness. A tension I couldn't explain. I lived in a constant state of alertness, bracing for impact even when nothing was wrong. Peace felt temporary, almost suspicious. If a season felt good, I immediately wondered when it would fall apart. I would imagine worst-case scenarios involving my husband or my children, playing them out in my mind as if preparing for tragedy would somehow soften the blow.

Underneath the anxiety was something harder to admit.

Bitterness.

I had spent years trying to understand my parents. I had extended grace. I had reminded myself that broken people often break others. But now that I was a mother myself, something shifted. I could not reconcile how they had not fought harder for us. I could not imagine choosing anything over my children. The compassion I once held for my father began mixing with resentment. Even in his death, I found myself grieving not just who he was, but who he never became.

That internal conflict began spilling into everything. I was short-tempered in moments that didn't deserve it. Emotionally distant without meaning to be. I realized I could no longer carry the weight quietly.

So I did what I have always done when I need clarity. I started writing.

Not for an audience. Not with structure or polish. Just pages filled with raw truth. I wrote about childhood memories I had never processed. About anger I had buried under responsibility. About grief that had never fully been named. The words were messy, but they were honest. And something about seeing them on paper made them feel less powerful over me.

Around that same time, we began preparing to sell our trailer.

We had lived there for nearly fifteen years. That home had held our earliest years of marriage. It had sheltered siblings we raised and babies we brought home. It had seen arguments, reconciliations, milestones, and miracles. It was more than a structure. It was proof of endurance.

But it was also aging. Something was always breaking. We were constantly patching, repairing, maintaining. We sensed it was time for something new, not out of greed or pride, but out of readiness. We poured ourselves into getting it ready to sell. Fresh paint. New appliances. Repairs that had been postponed for years. We listed it with hopeful hearts.

And then we waited.

Weeks passed. Then months. Nothing.

The waiting stirred insecurity in me. Maybe this wasn't God's plan. Maybe we were meant to stay there forever. Maybe wanting something new meant I was ungrateful. I wrestled with the difference between contentment and settling.

One Wednesday night during worship, I reached a breaking point. The music was playing, voices filling the sanctuary, but I couldn't sing. Tears streamed down my face as I stood there silently. I had been gripping control so tightly, trying to force movement. Finally, under my breath, I said, "Lord, if it's time, open the door. If it's not, close it. I release it."

I meant it.

For the first time, I loosened my grip. And in that surrender, something shifted internally. Not externally. The house hadn't sold. But the anxiety surrounding it softened. I stopped obsessing over timelines. I let go of trying to orchestrate outcomes.

During that season of waiting, life continued unfolding around us. My younger brother got married. My husband was asked to pray over him and his bride before their vows. As he stood beside my brother, hand resting on his shoulder, speaking words of blessing and protection, I felt something sacred in that moment. The little boy I once helped raise was now stepping into his own covenant. And the man who had walked through every storm with me was now standing in that fatherly gap once again.

It was a reminder that God redeems what feels missing.

Not long after, everything changed.

We found the house.

It checked every box we had quietly prayed over. Move-in ready. In a neighborhood where the kids could feel safe. Enough space without being excessive. It felt almost too aligned. I kept waiting for something to go wrong.

At the same time, we lowered the price on our trailer. Within days, we received an offer.

The sellers of the new house had multiple buyers interested. And yet, they chose us.

I remember asking God, almost in disbelief, "Why us?" Somewhere deep inside, I had convinced myself that blessings of that magnitude were for other families. Other stories. But God does not measure worth the way we do.

A few weeks after moving in, I was upstairs cleaning the boys' bedroom. The windows were open. Sunlight poured across the floor. The house was quiet in that sacred way homes sometimes are when life is simply steady.

I stopped mid-task and looked around.

This was ours.

Not just the walls. The peace.

I dropped to my knees right there on the bedroom floor. Tears streamed down my face as I whispered, "Thank You." Not for the square footage. Not for the upgrades. But for the journey.

For the timing.

For the seasons of waiting that shaped my trust.

For the reminder that surrender does not mean loss.

In that moment, I understood something clearly. God's goodness is not always loud. Sometimes it looks like stability. Sometimes it looks like sunlight through open windows. Sometimes it looks like a nervous system finally able to rest.

He had carried me through trauma, grief, anxiety, postpartum darkness, responsibility beyond my years. He had sustained our marriage, strengthened our family, and grown a business from prayer and perseverance.

And now He had given us a place to breathe.

This home was not proof that life would never hurt again. It was proof that healing was happening. That joy and sorrow can coexist. That waiting seasons are not wasted seasons.

For the first time in a long time, I felt rooted.

Not because everything was perfect.

But because I trusted the One who had led us there.

Chapter 23

When Love Isn't Enough

What felt like a new beginning for our family didn't take long to be tested.

One of my sisters found herself in a season of deep struggle. Her relationship was unstable, her world felt fragile, and before long, she and her longtime boyfriend lost custody of their daughter. No one enters motherhood planning for that kind of heartbreak. And no one loses a child without something inside them breaking.

I watched her trying to hold everything together while everything seemed to slip through her hands.

At one point, she became critically ill and was rushed to the hospital with sepsis. When my husband and I arrived, a nurse quietly told us she had come in just in time. I remember standing beside her bed, looking at how small she seemed in that hospital room, and feeling that old familiar fear rise up in my chest — the fear of losing someone you love before you're ready.

In moments like that, nothing else matters. Not frustration. Not history. Not disagreement. Just life.

For a while, it seemed like that health scare might mark a turning point. She began entering treatment programs and talking about rebuilding her life. She spoke about wanting stability, about wanting something different. I saw glimpses of hope in her. I held onto those glimpses tightly.

But change is rarely linear.

Over the next year, she entered several programs, yet never completed them. Each time she left early, I felt the air leave my lungs. I didn't always understand her decisions, and I won't pretend I did. I just knew I loved her and wanted her safe.

When she had nowhere else to go, she stayed with us. Our basement became her temporary landing place more than once. I laid down boundaries gently but firmly. If she stayed in our home, there had to be forward movement — some step toward health, toward stability. She agreed. I drove her to enrollments. I prayed in parking lots before dropping her off. I hoped each time would be the one that stuck.

But slowly, I began to unravel.

Not because I didn't love her.

But because I was trying to carry something that wasn't mine to carry.

I lost sleep listening for movement downstairs. I carried tension into my marriage without meaning to. My children felt the shift in the atmosphere even when we tried to protect them from it. I began to realize how quickly love can turn into responsibility, and how easily responsibility can become control.

I wanted to fix it. I wanted to protect her from repeating our past. I wanted to outrun generational pain by sheer will. Somewhere along the way, I had confused loving her with saving her.

One night, after another difficult conversation and another early departure from a program, I sat alone in the dark and admitted something I had been resisting: I could not transform her life for her.

I could support her.

I could pray for her.

I could love her.

But I could not do the inner work she had to choose for herself.

That surrender was painful. It felt like letting go of the future I had been trying to orchestrate. But it was also freeing. I stopped confusing love with control. I stopped believing that if I just tried harder, everything would change.

Years ago, a doctor once said something to me that didn't fully land at the time. He asked, "What is normal?" Back then, it felt like a passing comment. But in this season, that question came back to me with weight.

What is normal?

Who decides what healing is supposed to look like?

Who sets the timeline for growth?

Who determines where someone "should" be by now?

For a long time, I carried expectations — of what recovery should look like, of what stability should mean, of how quickly progress should happen. But I began to see that sometimes our expectations can become another burden for someone who is already struggling.

I no longer measure her life against where I think she should be.

I simply entrust it to God.

Letting go did not mean withdrawing love. It meant protecting my marriage and my children while keeping my heart open. It meant trusting that God loves her even more than I do. It meant believing that He is capable of working in ways I cannot see.

Today, she has a place of her own and is building her life in her own way. We are not as close as we once were, and that carries a quiet ache. But I still care about her deeply. I still pray for her. I still believe that God is writing chapters neither of us can fully see yet.

Our story is not finished.

This season taught me something I will never forget: love is powerful, but it is not sovereign. Only God transforms hearts. Only God writes the full story.

And sometimes the most faithful thing you can do is release your expectations, keep your heart soft, and trust that He is still at work — even when you cannot see the outcome.

    I still pray for her.

    And I trust that the same grace that met me in my own broken places continues reaching for her too.

Chapter 24

The Sister I Couldn't Save

M andy had always been more than my sister. We were only eleven months apart, but it felt like we shared one heartbeat. She was my childhood companion, my best friend, the one who knew every version of me before the world did. When she was scared at night, I held her hand until she fell asleep. If she thought she heard something outside, I was the one who got up to check. For as long as I can remember, I believed it was my job to protect her.

So when she found herself trapped in an abusive relationship, something inside me shifted into survival mode again.

I saw the fear in her eyes. I saw the way she flinched at raised voices. I saw her shrinking, piece by piece. I knew what control looked like. I knew how manipulation worked. And I could not stand by and watch it consume her.

When she said she was ready to leave, we moved quickly. My husband agreed to let her and her two boys stay in our basement while she rebuilt her life. The only condition was distance from him. She promised she would cut contact. I believed her because I needed to.

We drove to Arkansas, packed her apartment, and brought her home.

For a little while, it felt hopeful. The boys enrolled in school alongside my kids. Our house became loud and full in a new way. It was messy and imperfect, but there was structure. There was safety. I let myself imagine that maybe this was the turning point.

But abuse doesn't loosen its grip easily.

Phone calls resumed. Then secret conversations. Then weekend trips. I could feel the unraveling before I could prove it. The peace in our home grew fragile. My husband saw it too. She could feel that we were worried. That we didn't agree with some of her choices. We never had a dramatic confrontation, but the distance between us quietly grew. Not long after, she started looking for an apartment. And soon, she moved out.

After that, her life felt unpredictable. There were new plans, new hopes, new relationships. At one point, she believed she had found financial security in an unexpected arrangement overseas. Later, she reconnected with someone from her past and seemed genuinely happy for a brief moment. Each time she tried something new, I wanted to believe it was the beginning of something stable.

But the man she had been trying to escape never fully released his hold.

The violence escalated. One weekend, he beat her unconscious. The police were called. He was arrested. I thought, surely, this is the breaking point. Surely this is the moment she will never go back.

Three weeks later, she went to see him again.

That was the last time I heard from her.

She left her boys with our mom and drove to Arkansas. Hours passed. Calls went unanswered. We tried not to panic. We told ourselves there was an explanation. But by that evening, something felt wrong in my bones.

When my sister called me, hysterical, after finding a state report describing a fatality involving a vehicle like Mandy's, the world around me went silent. I remember collapsing to the floor. I couldn't breathe. I couldn't process. I just kept saying no.

There are moments in life when your body understands something before your mind can accept it.

That was one of them.

Waiting for confirmation was unbearable. The police needed identifying information. DNA. Details no sister should ever have to provide. We moved forward with arrangements while still clinging to a thin thread of denial.

On Friday, my husband and I picked out her casket. I don't know how I walked through that process. I don't know how I stood upright. I just know that I did, because someone had to.

The confirmation came later.

It was her.

We buried her on Easter Sunday at the foot of our father's grave. The symbolism was not lost on me. So much pain in one family plot. So much unfinished history.

The hardest part of all of it was telling her boys.

There are no words for that moment. No script. No gentle version of that truth. I remember holding them as they cried, feeling their small bodies shake, wishing I could absorb their grief into my own and spare them from it.

The sound of their cries still echoes in me.

For a long time afterward, guilt followed me everywhere.

Had I done enough?

Had I pushed harder?

Had I prayed harder?

Could I have forced her to stay away?

Those questions became a quiet torment.

But eventually, I had to face the truth I had been learning in pieces for years: some battles cannot be fought from the outside. They must be fought and won from within. I could offer safety. I could offer love. I could offer a home. But I could not override her choices.

That realization broke something in me.

One afternoon, weeks after the funeral, I sat alone on the back porch and let myself finally speak to God without trying to be strong. I didn't ask why. I didn't bargain. I just cried. And in that quiet surrender, I felt something steady settle over me. Not answers. Not understanding. Just presence.

Mandy's life was complicated. She searched for love in places that hurt her. She gave more than she received. She longed for stability but struggled to hold onto it.

I will always wish the story ended differently.

But I believe this: the love she searched for her whole life is the love she now knows fully. A love that does not manipulate. A love that does not abandon. A love that does not harm.

Even in our deepest grief, God does not leave us.

Even when the ending shatters us, He remains steady.

I could not save my sister.

But I trust that God holds her now in ways I never could.

And on the days when the ache feels fresh again, that is the truth I cling to.

Chapter 25

Carried Through the Breaking

Gaining custody of my sister's boys was not a difficult decision. It was simply the right one.

They had already been woven into our lives for years. They were part of our routines, our holidays, our everyday moments. Weekend visits turned into school pickups. Sunday dinners turned into extended stays. To anyone outside looking in, they might have seemed like extended family. But to us, they were already deeply connected to our home. Still, nothing truly prepares you for the shift from helping to raising.

They had just lost their mother. Grief followed them into our house in ways that were quiet and in ways that were loud. Familiar spaces suddenly felt permanent. What once felt temporary now carried weight. They came carrying confusion, trauma, and survival instincts shaped by instability. We welcomed them fully, but we understood that this transition would change the dynamic of our entire family.

At that point in our lives, we had finally reached a season that felt steady. After years of raising my siblings and navigating constant responsibility, things had calmed. Our four children were growing. My business was stable. Our marriage had found a rhythm again. For the first time in a long time, life felt settled. We could breathe.

And then we chose to stretch again.

We did not hesitate, but that does not mean it was easy. The house grew louder. Bedtimes became flexible. Emotional outbursts required patience we did not always have. Structure, which had once brought peace to our home, became harder to maintain. I softened in places where I had once been strict because I knew I was not just parenting behavior. I was navigating grief.

My own children noticed the differences. They were honest about it. They felt the shift in attention. They saw that I responded differently to certain behaviors. They were not wrong. I was trying to make room for healing while still protecting stability, and that balance is difficult to maintain under one roof.

My husband and I were doing the best we knew how to. We were still young parents ourselves. We were trying to discipline while also understanding trauma. There were moments we were too strict because we were overwhelmed.

There were moments we bent too much because we felt compassion. We did not always get it right. We were learning in real time.

The weight of responsibility began to show in subtle ways. Our conversations became more logistical. Date nights became rare. The days felt long and full. We were not falling apart, but we were tired.

Around a year into the transition, my body began to show signs that something was not right. What I first assumed was normal exhaustion slowly turned into persistent pain. My joints ached. My muscles felt inflamed. Fatigue settled in deeply and did not lift, even after rest. I kept pushing through it the way I had always pushed through everything else in my life, until I simply could not anymore.

After multiple appointments and bloodwork, I was told that my ANA levels were positive. More testing followed. Eventually, the rheumatologist diagnosed me with Undifferentiated Connective Tissue Disease and Fibromyalgia. I was thirty-six years old.

Hearing those words forced me to confront something I had avoided for years. I had lived in a constant state of responsibility since I was a teenager. I had carried more than I realized. My body had absorbed stress, grief, hypervigilance, and pressure for decades. Now it was asking for something I had rarely allowed myself: rest.

I stepped away from work for six weeks. It was not an easy decision. Rest felt unfamiliar and uncomfortable.

I was used to moving, fixing, providing, doing. Sitting still felt unnatural. But slowly, in the quiet of those weeks, I began to understand that slowing down was not weakness. It was necessary.

With the house quieter during school hours, I started spending intentional time in prayer again. I walked through the rooms, praying over each bed, asking God to protect our children and to bring healing where I could not. I prayed for my nephews as they adjusted. I prayed for my marriage. I prayed for strength I did not feel.

Gradually, the atmosphere in our home began to soften. The tension eased. The boys found more stability in routine. My children felt more of my presence again. I began to recognize that healing was happening slowly, not because I was forcing it, but because I had finally stopped trying to control everything.

I also began to accept something important. I could not save everyone. I could not undo trauma. I could not carry every burden without consequence. But I could create a home where love was consistent and where growth was possible.

There are still difficult days. My health continues to require awareness and boundaries. I have had to learn to pace myself in ways I never had before. But there is peace in that pacing. There is wisdom in recognizing limits.

God did not allow my body to slow down as punishment. He used it to teach me how to live differently.

To release what was never mine to carry alone. To depend on Him in a deeper way.

The restoration in our home did not happen overnight. It came through surrender. Through rest. Through humility. Through learning that strength is not always about endurance, but about knowing when to step back.

And in that season of stillness, I found God again in a way that felt steady and sustaining. Not dramatic. Not loud. Just faithful.

He did not remove the responsibility.

He walked with me through it.

And that made all the difference.

Chapter 26

Letting Go of the Hurt

During the season when my health was at its worst, when climbing the stairs left me breathless and the pain in my body felt constant and unrelenting, one of my siblings reached out to our mom. She had watched me slowly unravel under the weight of everything I was carrying. The exhaustion that never lifted. The business that still needed attention. Six kids under one roof. Grief that seemed to sit just beneath the surface of every day. For the first time, someone said what I had been too proud to admit: I shouldn't have to do this alone.

She called our mom and offered to help her move to Alabama. She told her she would help financially, that she would make it work, that I needed her close. And in a moment of what I can only describe as vulnerable honesty, my mom said yes.

That single word stirred something in me I had buried years ago. For a brief and fragile moment, I let myself believe she finally saw me. I allowed myself to imagine what it might feel like to have her nearby, not as a visitor, but as part of our everyday life. I didn't need her to fix anything. I didn't expect her to carry my burdens. I just wanted her presence. A ride to the doctor on a hard day. A grandmother who showed up without being asked. A simple hug when I felt overwhelmed. It awakened a longing I had spent most of my life trying to silence.

But just as quickly as she had agreed, she changed her mind. She told me they could not leave her mother-in-law because she needed them. And just like that, the door quietly closed.

It should not have surprised me. I had spent most of my life lowering expectations so I would not be hurt. I had told myself over and over that she was who she was, and I could not make her become something she was not. But this time I had allowed hope in, and hope makes disappointment sharper. It was not really about her moving. It was about what it represented. It was another reminder that even in my sickness, even in my exhaustion, I was still expected to hold everything together. I was still the strong one. Still the capable one. Still the one who did not "need" anything.

We continued talking. She still visited. On the surface, nothing changed. But internally, something shifted in me. I could feel it whenever her name appeared on my phone. A tightness in my chest. A heaviness in my stomach. It was not anger. It was grief. Grief for the mother I longed for. Grief for the relationship that never quite formed the way I needed it to. Grief for the little girl in me who kept hoping that one day she would finally feel chosen.

One night around two in the morning, I woke up with that weight pressing on me. The house was quiet. Everyone asleep. I slipped out of bed and knelt beside it, and for the first time in a long time, I let myself cry without holding it together. I told God I was tired. Tired of carrying everyone. Tired of fighting for relationships that never felt equal. Tired of needing something that might never come. I told Him I forgave her again. Not just for this moment, but for years of unmet expectations. I released the hope that she would one day become who I needed her to be.

The situation did not change overnight. She did not suddenly move closer. Nothing dramatic happened. But something inside of me softened. Peace came, not because the relationship was repaired, but because I stopped trying to force it into something it was never going to be.

That night, I picked up my phone and sent her a simple message telling her I loved her. Not because she had earned it or because anything had shifted between us, but because I had changed. I no longer needed her to be different in order for me to be whole.

I am learning that forgiveness does not always look like reconciliation. Sometimes it looks like boundaries. Sometimes it looks like loving someone without giving them full access to your heart. Sometimes it means accepting that people can only give from what they have, and if they do not have it, no amount of longing will create it.

Letting go does not mean forgetting. It means freeing myself from the constant ache of expecting someone to fill a space only God ever truly could. And in that release, I found relief. Not because I finally had the mother I wanted, but because I finally stopped waiting for her to become someone she was not.

In that surrender, I felt God meet me again, steady and faithful as He has always been. And for the first time in a long time, I felt lighter.

Chapter 27

Peace in the Aftermath

Each of my siblings has found their own way. When I look at them now—raising their children, building marriages, making choices that reflect strength instead of survival—I feel something I didn't always believe was possible. Gratitude. We were once just kids trying to make it through another day, navigating chaos we didn't create. Now we are adults creating stability for the next generation. That shift alone feels like a miracle. We did not just escape our past; we learned from it. We did not just survive it; we grew beyond it.

One of my greatest joys now is hosting the holidays. My home fills with siblings, nieces, nephews, cousins, and the kind of noise that only comes from children who feel safe. The kitchen stays crowded. The living room overflows. Laughter echoes down the hallway. I often pause in the middle of it all just to take it in. There was a time when our family gatherings were unpredictable and tense. Now they feel rooted. Watching the younger generation run freely through my home reminds me that the sacrifices were not wasted. Something steady was planted in the middle of all that brokenness, and now I get to see it grow.

It has not erased the past. There are still moments when memories surface unexpectedly. There are still conversations that carry weight. But when I look at the lives my siblings are building, I see resilience where there once was fear. I see intention where there once was reaction. I see faith that was shaped through hardship, not handed down easily. That gives me hope for my own children too. I imagine the day they step into adulthood fully aware of who they are and where they come from, but no longer defined by it. I picture holding my grandchildren someday and knowing that the years of endurance, the sleepless nights, the prayers whispered through exhaustion, all of it mattered.

Life today looks different than those early years. I returned to work, but only three days a week. I learned that sustainability matters more than proving I can handle everything. My business continues, but it no longer consumes me. I plan around school schedules and sports practices. I listen when my body signals that it needs rest. I used to equate slowing down with weakness. Now I understand it as wisdom. Peace requires margin, and margin requires boundaries.

The boys have grown in ways that once felt uncertain. Their grief is still part of their story, but it no longer overshadows who they are becoming. In the early days, I worried constantly about whether they would ever feel steady again. Their pain was visible, raw, unpredictable. But healing does not always happen dramatically. It happens slowly, in routines, in laughter, in safe conversations, in consistency. I see it now when they talk about their mom with both sadness and warmth. I see it when they move forward without carrying shame. God has done work in their hearts that I could never have forced.

There are still tender days. Birthdays and holidays bring a quiet weight. But those moments have shifted. Instead of only sorrow, there is remembrance. Instead of only pain, there is honor. We speak her name openly. We tell stories. We allow both grief and gratitude to exist in the same room.

My marriage remains one of the greatest testimonies of God's faithfulness in my life. Danny and I recently celebrated twenty years together. In the early seasons of raising children and carrying responsibilities far beyond our years, that milestone felt distant and almost unrealistic. There were years when our relationship was built more on commitment than convenience, more on perseverance than ease. We were partners in survival long before we had the luxury of slowing down to simply enjoy each other. Recently, we took five days away together out west. Just the two of us. No schedules. No logistics. Just space to remember who we are beyond the roles we fill. That time reminded me that what we have is not fragile. It is anchored.

When I look back over everything—the trauma, the grief, the illnesses, the disappointments, the unexpected turns—I see a thread that never broke. God was present in every season. Not always loudly. Not always in the ways I wanted. But consistently. Even in the moments when I questioned Him, even when I felt abandoned or exhausted, He was steady.

There were times I truly believed I could not endure one more crisis. Times when I said out loud, "I cannot do this again." But the truth is, I was never meant to do it alone. God's grace filled the gaps I could not cover. His strength carried what my body and heart could not. His peace guarded my home when anxiety tried to take root again.

I no longer feel the need to control every outcome. I no longer feel responsible for everyone's choices. I have learned that peace does not come from everything going right. It comes from trusting the One who holds it all together. I do not have all the answers, and I am finally comfortable with that.

This life is not perfect. It is layered. It carries both joy and memory, both gratitude and scars. But it is sacred. It is full of grace. And when I sit in the quiet of my home, listening to the hum of everyday life, I feel something I once thought might always be out of reach.

Stability.
Not because life stopped being complicated.
But because God remained faithful through it all.
And that is enough.

Chapter 28

A Call To Know Christ

If you have made it this far in my story, I want you to understand something clearly. None of this was written to highlight my strength. It was written to point to the One who carried me when I had none. Every chapter, every memory, every painful confession has one purpose behind it: to show what Jesus can do with a life that is surrendered to Him.

There were many moments in my life when I could have let bitterness take over. Moments when I could have hardened completely. I have known trauma, abandonment, regret, and exhaustion at levels that felt unbearable. I have faced grief that stole my breath and responsibility that felt heavier than my body could carry. There were seasons when I did not feel strong. There were days I did not feel faithful. There were nights I did not even know how to pray.

But even then, I was not alone.

I did not survive because I am resilient. I survived because Christ met me in my weakness. The peace that steadied me was not something I manufactured. It was not tied to circumstances improving or pain disappearing. It was a quiet assurance that no matter what was unraveling around me, God had not stepped away.

Jesus once said, "Peace I leave with you; my peace I give you. I do not give to you as the world gives." I did not understand that verse when I was younger. I do now. The world's version of peace depends on comfort, control, and predictable outcomes. God's peace remains even when none of those things are present.

Faith did not remove my struggles. It transformed the way I walked through them.

And here is the truth I want you to hear: feeling regret is not the same as surrender. Wanting things to be different is not the same as giving your life to Christ. Transformation begins when we stop managing our own brokenness and place it fully in His hands. God does not ask for perfection. He asks for your heart.

Jeremiah 29 says that when we seek Him with all our heart, we will find Him. I have found that to be true. Not because I deserved it. Not because I earned it. But because He is faithful.

The gospel is not about religion or performance. It is about rescue. "For God so loved the world that He gave His only Son." That love is not abstract. It is personal. Jesus carried our sin, our shame, and our wounds to the cross.

He rose again so that we would not be defined by what broke us.

Maybe as you read this book, you saw pieces of yourself in my story. Maybe you recognized patterns in your own life that feel impossible to escape. Addiction. Anger. Control. Fear. Maybe you are exhausted from trying to outrun your past or prove your worth.

You do not have to keep living that way.

In Christ, you are not just improved. You are made new. Scripture says, "If anyone is in Christ, he is a new creation." That promise is not poetic language. It is real. It means the story you were born into does not have to be the story you pass on. Generational cycles can end. Shame can lose its grip. Healing can begin.

Following Jesus does not mean your life becomes easy. It means you no longer walk alone. It means your suffering is not wasted. It means your identity is anchored in something stronger than your circumstances.

I am free today not because I did everything right, but because Jesus saved me. He is still shaping me, still correcting me, still teaching me to trust Him more deeply. Faith is not a one-time moment. It is a daily surrender.

If you feel something stirring in your heart right now, do not ignore it. You do not need polished words or perfect understanding. You simply need willingness.

You can pray something like this:

"Jesus, I need You. I believe You are the Son of God. I believe You died for my sins and rose again. Forgive me. Change me. Teach me to trust You. I give You my life."

It does not have to sound impressive. It just has to be real.

If you prayed that prayer, this is the beginning, not the end. Find a Bible. Find a church that teaches truth. Surround yourself with people who will encourage your faith. You will stumble at times. We all do. But grace will meet you there.

You are not too far gone. You are not too broken. You are not disqualified by your past.

If my story shows anything, I hope it shows this: God still writes redemption stories. And He is not finished yet.

Epilogue

She Made It

Sometimes I think about that little girl.

The one who climbed into her baby sister's crib because she was scared of the dark.

The one who learned too early how to stay quiet, how to protect others, how to carry more than she should.

The one who felt different from the other kids. Older somehow. Heavier somehow.

She didn't know how her story would unfold. She didn't know there would be courtrooms and funerals and sleepless nights. She didn't know she would one day raise siblings, bury a sister, fight through illness, and still stand.

She just knew how to survive.

If I could sit beside her now, I wouldn't tell her all the details of what's ahead. I wouldn't overwhelm her with the storms she'll face. I would simply take her small hands in mine and tell her this:

You are going to make it.
Not because life will be easy.
Not because people won't disappoint you.
Not because you'll avoid heartbreak.
You will make it because God will never leave you.

There will be moments you feel abandoned. Moments you question everything. Moments you believe you are too tired to keep going. But grace will meet you there. Again and again.

One day you will stand in a home filled with laughter. You will host holidays instead of hiding from chaos. You will watch children run freely through rooms that feel safe. You will sit beside a husband who stayed. You will feel peace in a way you never thought possible.

And you will realize something beautiful.

The little girl who learned how to survive grew into a woman who learned how to heal.

The cycles did not win.

The trauma did not define you.

The pain did not get the final word.

God did.

If you are reading this and you see yourself in that little girl, I want you to hear it too:

You are not stuck in the story you were handed.

There is more ahead of you than what's behind you.

And the same God who carried me will carry you.

We made it.

And by His grace, so will you.

Acknowledgments

First and foremost, I thank God for His relentless faithfulness. Every chapter of this book exists because of His grace.

To my family, thank you for walking through the hard seasons with me and celebrating the joyful ones. Our story is intertwined, and I cherish that.

To my husband, Danny, thank you for standing beside me through storms we never saw coming. Your steadiness has been one of God's greatest gifts in my life.

To my daughter, Alissa, thank you for helping shape this manuscript with your time and care. Watching you step into your own gifts has been a joy.

And to you, the reader, thank you for trusting me with your time and your heart. My prayer is that you close this book knowing that no matter what you have lived through, hope is not out of reach.

With gratitude,
Misty Fields

www.ingramcontent.com/pod-product-compliance
Lightning Source LLC
Chambersburg PA
CBHW050522100526
44581CB00002B/75